Chile

WORLD BIBLIOGRAPHICAL SERIES

General Editors:
Robert L. Collison (Editor-in-chief)

John J. Horton   Ian Wallace
Hans H. Wellisch   Ralph Lee Woodward, Jr.

Robert L. Collison (Editor-in-chief) is Professor emeritus, Library and Information Studies, University of California, Los Angeles, and was a President of the Society of Indexers. Following the war, he served as Reference Librarian for the City of Westminster and later became Librarian to the BBC. During his fifty years as a professional librarian in England and the USA, he has written more than twenty works on bibliography, librarianship, indexing and related subjects.

John J. Horton is Deputy Librarian of the University of Bradford and currently Chairman of its Academic Board of Studies in Social Sciences. He has maintained a longstanding interest in the discipline of area studies and its associated bibliographical problems, with special reference to European Studies. In particular he has published in the field of Icelandic and of Yugoslav studies, including the two relevant volumes in the World Bibliographical Series.

Ian Wallace is Professor of Modern Languages at Loughborough University of Technology. A graduate of Oxford in French and German, he also studied in Tübingen, Heidelberg and Lausanne before taking teaching posts at universities in the USA, Scotland and England. He specializes in East German affairs, especially literature and culture, on which he has published numerous articles and books. In 1979 he founded the journal *GDR Monitor*, which he continues to edit.

Hans H. Wellisch is Professor emeritus at the College of Library and Information Services, University of Maryland. He was President of the American Society of Indexers and was a member of the International Federation for Documentation. He is the author of numerous articles and several books on indexing and abstracting, and has published *The Conversion of Scripts* and *Indexing and Abstracting: an International Bibliography*. He also contributes frequently to *Journal of the American Society for Information Science, The Indexer* and other professional journals.

Ralph Lee Woodward, Jr. is Chairman of the Department of History at Tulane University, New Orleans, where he has been Professor of History since 1970. He is the author of *Central America, a Nation Divided*, 2nd ed. (1985), as well as several monographs and more than sixty scholarly articles on modern Latin America. He has also compiled volumes in the World Bibliographical Series on *Belize* (1980), *Nicaragua* (1983), and *El Salvador* (forthcoming). Dr. Woodward edited the Central American section of the *Research Guide to Central America and the Caribbean* (1985) and is currently editor of the Central American history section of the *Handbook of Latin American Studies*.

VOLUME 97

Chile

Harold Blakemore
Compiler

CLIO PRESS
OXFORD, ENGLAND · SANTA BARBARA, CALIFORNIA
DENVER, COLORADO

British Library Cataloguing in Publication Data

Blakemore, Harold, *1930*-
Chile.—(World bibliographical
series; v.97).
1. Chile, to 1988. Bibliographies
I. Title   II. Series
016.983

ISBN 1–85109–026–6

Clio Press Ltd.,
55 St. Thomas' Street,
Oxford OX1 1JG, England.

ABC-Clio Information Services,
Riviera Campus, 2040 Alameda Padre Serra,
Santa Barbara, CA. 93103, USA.

Designed by Bernard Crossland
Typeset by Columns Design and Production Services, Reading, England
Printed and bound in Great Britain by
Billing and Sons Ltd., Worcester.

THE WORLD BIBLIOGRAPHICAL SERIES

This series, which is principally designed for the English speaker, will eventually cover every country in the world, each in a separate volume comprising annotated entries on works dealing with its history, geography, economy and politics; and with its people, their culture, customs, religion and social organization. Attention will also be paid to current living conditions – housing, education, newspapers, clothing, etc. – that are all too often ignored in standard bibliographies; and to those particular aspects relevant to individual countries. Each volume seeks to achieve, by use of careful selectivity and critical assessment of the literature, an expression of the country and an appreciation of its nature and national aspirations, to guide the reader towards an understanding of its importance. The keynote of the series is to provide, in a uniform format, an interpretation of each country that will express its culture, its place in the world, and the qualities and background that make it unique.

VOLUMES IN THE SERIES

Contents

Contents

Contents

Introduction

Despite its comparatively modest size as a South American state, covering 626,756 square kilometres, excluding Chilean Antarctica, and with a population of only 12,500,000, Chile has attracted a disproportionate share of world attention since the 1960s. The reasons for this are essentially political. Against its earlier history as an independent state from the early nineteenth century, and as a republic which, in contrast to most of its Spanish American neighbours, evolved a functioning, constitutional, multi-party system of government at an early date, its reputation was enhanced when the people, in democratic elections, chose the first Christian Democratic president in the continent in 1964, and the first Marxist president in 1970. In 1973, however, in a situation of increasing economic and political breakdown, the armed services took over government, broke sharply with tradition and, much to the surprise of most observers, have remained in power to the time of writing. It was that break, and the highly autocratic, not to say repressive, nature of the current régime which put Chile into the international spotlight, an unusual position for a country so remote from geopolitical considerations.

Prior to these events, however, among those who knew the continent, Chile already had a distinctive reputation for orderly government. Founded as Spain's most far-flung colony in the 1540s, by Pedro de Valdivia, Chile had, at the time of independence, nearly three hundred years later, advantages that few other states possessed. Today, covering, from north to south, a distance of over 4,200 km. and, at its widest, nowhere more than 400 km., it is one of the most peculiarly shaped countries in the world. However, for 300 years it was only a third of its present size, confined to a compact block of territory with almost perfect naturally defined frontiers: to the west the Pacific ocean, to the east the high mountains of the Andes, to the north the

Introduction

Atacama desert, and to the south the river Bio-Bio, providing a natural frontier between Spanish Chile and hostile Indian territory.

This compact shape helped to create a higher degree of unity than in most other Spanish American colonies, and this was paralleled by a comparatively simple racial structure. The natives of the central valley had been absorbed into the society of the white settlers, so that, by independence, there were really only two races, whites and *mestizos*, the products of white-Indian fusion. Socially, a close-knit landed oligarchy ruled all branches of the national life while an illiterate peasantry obeyed.

After the turbulence of the wars of independence and their aftermath, when men and groups jostled for power, the country settled into a constitutional mould, through the political realism of its leaders, backed by the constitution of 1833 which, though amended, survived, largely, until 1925. In the nineteenth century, the economy grew, resting on the twin pillars of agriculture and mining, with the fertility of the land matched by the richness of its mineral resources. In the 1880s, a contemporary observer of Chile described it as 'the model republic of South America'. Between 1833 and 1924 only three attempts were made to change the constitutional order by force and, although one succeeded, in 1891, that changed the nature of government, rather than its form: orderly habits in politics had been well-established.

At the same time, Chile had become the hegemonic power on the Pacific coast of South America, largely through its naval strength. Chile won both wars that it fought against Bolivia and Peru in the 1830s and 1880s, securing additional territory and mineral wealth, as well as the accolade of the more developed nations of the world.

The social structure, however, had remained largely intact. It was dominated by a small oligarchy at the apex, with the broad base of the masses below. However, with the growth of the economy, the beginnings of new middle social groups, the rise of a genuine proletariat, and, not least, the expansion of population, urbanization and education, a challenge was posed to the old order with demands for greater political participation by those still largely excluded, and a more equitable distribution of the national wealth. With an export economy, the country was exposed to external shocks such as the First World War and the depression of the late 1920s and early 1930s. The former ushered in a turbulent period, culminating in military intervention in 1924-25, and a 'constitutional' quasi-dictatorship (that of Carlos

Ibáñez) from 1927-31. His fall, largely the result of the impact of
the depression, saw Chile return to its normal constitutional
manners, with parties competing for political power at the ballot
box.

That tradition, once restored, lasted until 1973. The military
government which came to power then has been much more
dictatorial than that of Ibáñez, whose régime was mild-mannered
compared with other dictatorships in Latin America. It has
initiated economic policies of free enterprize which are in stark
contrast to the state-interventionist policies of the previous five
decades. What Chile's future may be is a matter of conjecture,
but there is no question of its distinctive nature in the evolution
of the states of Latin America.

The bibliography

This is, inevitably, a *selective* bibliography. Throughout, an attempt
has been made to adhere to certain criteria of selection. First,
since the bibliography is aimed primarily at the non-specialist
English-speaking reader, the compiler has excluded a large
number of works in Spanish which, in a bibliography intended
simply for scholars, would and should have been included.
Inevitably, however, for certain disciplines and subjects, English-
language coverage is still thin, and Spanish-language works have
been included on these occasions for topics which, otherwise,
would have little or no coverage at all. Secondly, a deliberate
attempt has been made to include as much recent writing as
possible, though certain older items, such as classic travel
literature, merit inclusion. Also, while articles, as well as more
substantial works, are mentioned, the compiler has not thought it
worthwhile to include very short articles appearing in highly
specialized journals, such as those dealing with medicine, since
they do not seem appropriate for a selective bibliography for the
reader interested in Chile in general terms. Similarly, short
entries on Chile in encyclopaedias have been largely ignored,
except where no other recourse was possible.

To counterbalance these possible defects, the section on
bibliographies is reasonably comprehensive, to enable the
inquisitive or, indeed, the more specialized reader to research
more thoroughly.

The balance of subjects reflects the material available and the
criteria indicated. However, given the distinctive evolution of Chile
in its continental context, and the distinguished historiography of

Introduction

the republic, history predominates. Equally, the controversial character of more recent events, and the international attention they have attracted, means that near contemporary politics and economics command considerable space. It is hoped, however, that there is sufficient balance of subject coverage to cater for a wide, multi-disciplinary audience, and that the annotations provide a reasonable guide, not only to content but also to the particular author's point of view.

The map, given at the end of the bibliography, is also limited in scope. The reader is, therefore, advised to refer to the relevant sections within the bibliography for more detailed cartographical information.

The compiler has sought to steer that narrow course between the Scylla of error and the Charybdis of omission. Where he has failed, it is in no way due to the many people who have helped him. Invidious though it is, he wishes to record his gratitude to particular scholars and librarians for navigating him through unknown waters. Indebtedness must be acknowledged to the library of the Institute of Latin American Studies at the University of London, and particularly Alan Biggins; to that of the University itself, and notably to Pat Noble and Connie Hawkes, and to that of the Hispanic and Luzo-Brazilian Councils (Canning House) and its librarian, Noel Treacy. Catherine Boyle of Strathclyde University and John King of Warwick were indispensable on music, theatre, film and literature; Robert Gwynne of Birmingham on geographical aspects; Annette Barnard of Newcastle on education; Simon Collier of Essex on those epochs of Chilean history that are more his than mine; Tessa Cubitt of Portsmouth Polytechnic, Ricardo Couyoumdjian of the Catholic University of Chile and Bente Bittmann of Antofagasta for other helpful advice. Finally, Robert Neville of Clio Press, who gave meaning to collaboration. The prerogatives – and possibly penalties – of selectivity and subjectivity are mine, and mine alone.

Harold Blakemore
London
March 1988

xiv

The Country and Its People

1 **Chile. A country study.**
Edited by Andrew T. Merrill. Washington, DC: Government
Printing Office, 1982. 2nd ed. 294p. 5 maps. bibliog. (Area
Handbook Series prepared under the auspices of the Foreign Area
Studies Division, American University).
This is an up-dated, though shorter, useful and informative guide to both country
and people. The first edition (by Thomas E. Weil and others) appeared in 1969. It
is replete with basic information on institutions, social, political and economic,
etc., communications, including the media, geographical sketches and so on. It is
a good basic and factual introduction to Chile.

2 **Let's visit Chile.**
Gary Lyle. London: Burke, 1984. 96p. map.
A basic introductory book, embellished with some splendid photographs.

3 **Chile in pictures.**
Lois Bianchi. New York: Sterling, 1977. 64p. (Visual Geography
Series).
A good pictorial representation of Chile's extraordinary geographical diversity.

4 **Getting to know Chile.**
Jim Breetveld. London: Frederick Muller, 1962. 64p. 1 map.
('Getting To Know' Books).
Essentially aimed at the junior audience (ages 8-12), this is, despite its date, a
very compact, informative book about those aspects of Chile that remain constant
through changes of government – its history, people, cities, fauna, food, family
life and customs.

1

5 **The land and people of Chile.**
George Pendle. London: Black, 1960. 96p. bibliog. map. (Lands and Peoples Series).

Written essentially for senior school pupils, this is a well-illustrated and concisely-written introduction to Chile by a British businessman who had long acquaintance with Latin America and published a large number of highly-regarded books on the continent. Though written nearly thirty years ago, it can still be recommended as a basic text in schools.

6 **Chilean scrapbook.**
Stephen Clissold. London: Cresset, 1952. 316p. 4 maps.

The title of this book might lead the prospective reader to ignore it. That would be a mistake for it is, in fact, an excellent introduction to Chile, its regions and their people and its history to 1950. Detailed and nicely annotated, it is highly recommended to the layman wishing to learn much about Chile from one book.

7 **Chile. 1973-1983. Ten years of achievement.**
Santiago: Ministerio Secretaría General de Gobierno, 1983. 144p. 2 maps.

Although it is clearly a piece of propaganda to mark and praise the first decade of military rule, the book has two merits. Firstly, the text is bilingual (Spanish and English) and contains much accurate factual information and, secondly, it has a large number of splendid pictures in colour. These have been carefully chosen, for instance there are none of shanty-towns, but they do convey the scenic variety and wide-ranging resources of the country. The book is worth looking at, despite its purpose.

8 **Chile: un país, un pueblo.** (Chile: a country, a people.)
Jaime Valdés. Paris: Editions Delroisse, [n.d.] 164p.

The non-Spanish speaker will still find this general survey useful for its many colour illustrations.

9 **Carretera austral. Integración de Chile.** (Southern highway. The integration of Chile.)
George Munro. Santiago: Ediciones Servicios Promocionales, 1982. 73p.

This is a magnificent collection of colour photographs of the varied landscapes of south-central Chile, with the added advantage of captions in both Spanish and English.

10 **My native land. Panorama, reminiscences, writers and folklore.**
Agustín Edwards. London: Ernest Benn, 1928. bibliog. map.

Edwards, scion of one of the most distinguished Anglo-Chilean families, was Chilean ambassador to London for many years in the 1920s. Although this book was written at that time, its geographical description of Chile's regions, its historical anecdotes and its folkloric references have not dated. Edwards also wrote serious historical works and may be regarded as a man of extraordinary culture and knowledge of his native land.

11 **Image of Chile.**
Graeme Parish.   London: Charles Knight, 1972. 167p. map.
A genial account of Chile and its people by an Irish writer who knows both well. The historical approach gives depth to the interpretation of what was the contemporary scene when the book was written.

12 **Child in Chile.**
Bea Howe.   London: André Deutsch, 1957. 192p. bibliog.
A charmingly evocative account of the writer's childhood, spent in Valparaiso at the end of the last century and the beginning of this one. The local scene and characters at that time are beautifully captured.

13 **Sweet waters: a Chilean farm.**
C. J. Lambert.   Westport, Connecticutt: Greenwood, 1975. 212p. 2 maps.
Originally published in London in 1952, this is a reprint of a delightful description of life on a large estate in the Chilean central valley, evoking a period (the 1920s) before the turbulence of modern times. The author was directly descended from Charles Lambert, an Alsatian by origin, who made his fortune from copper in the early nineteenth century and invested some of it in land.

14 **We farmed a desert.**
E. B. Herivel.   London: Faber & Faber, 1957. 280p. 4 maps.
The writer, the sister of C. J. Lambert, provides an interesting autobiographical account of life on the farm her family owned and worked in the northern Huasco valley in the semi-arid region north of Santiago. The book contains a good deal of local colour and photographs.

15 **Easter Island: island of enigmas.**
John dos Passos.   Garden City, New York: Doubleday, 1971. 150p.
A popularized interpretation of the evolution of the island, annexed by Chile in the 1880s, which the well-known American writer visited. There are a number of illustrations.

16 **Man and environment in the south Chilean islands.**
M. W. Holdgate.   *Geographical Journal*, vol. 127, no. 4 (Dec. 1961), p. 401-16.
A solid account of a Royal Society expedition to southern Chile, describing the physical nature of the terrain, geology, vegetation etc., but which is, perhaps, more interesting for its treatment of the now much-reduced native tribes, the Ona, Yámana and Alacaluf. It is also concerned with European settlement patterns.

3

The Country and Its People

17 **Uttermost part of the earth.**
  E. Lucas Bridges.   London: Hodder & Stoughton, 1948. 558p.
  2 maps.

This provides one of the most detailed accounts of the native Indians of Tierra del Fuego and Patagonia, the Ona and Yaghan in particular. The author's father was a Christian missionary in the region from the 1870s to the end of the century, and this book is based on the son's extensive memoirs as well as further research. The tribes about whom he wrote are now virtually extinct and this picture of life among them is a classic of description and narrative.

18 **Patagonian panorama.**
  Tom P. Jones.   Bournemouth, England: Outspoken Press, 1961, 173p.

An autobiographical and highly evocative account of life in Chilean Patagonia by an Englishman who lived there from the 1900s to the 1950s. Though very anecdotal, it is, nonetheless, interesting.

Geography

General

19 **Chile: a geographic extravaganza.**
Benjamin Subercaseaux, translated from the Spanish by Angel
Flores. New York: Hafner, 1971. 255p.

Perhaps the best known popular work in Chilean geography, not least for its
poetic descriptive character. The chapter headings are far from conventional,
bearing titles such as 'Land of the tranquil mornings', 'Land of the snow-capped
wall' and 'Land of the blue mirrors', in dealing with Chile's extraordinary shape
and the diversity of its regions. It is a basic book.

20 **Chile.**
Harold Blakemore.   In: *Latin America: geographical perspectives*.
Edited by Harold Blakemore, Clifford T. Smith. London, New
York: Methuen, 1983. 2nd ed. p. 457-531. 2 maps. bibliog.

An essay on the historical geography of Chile, tracing the evolution of the
country's diverse regions and their economic development from the colonial
period to the present day. Blakemore emphasizes the dichotomy between the
centralist tradition of the Chilean state and the great variety of Chile's regions
from the desert north to the sub-Antarctic south.

21 **Geografía económica de Chile.** (Economic geography of Chile.)
Edited by Gemines, *Sociedad de Estudios Profesionales*.
Santiago: Editorial Andrés Bello, 1982. 1083p. bibliog.

Far and away the most encyclopaedic survey of Chilean economic geography,
with a large number of tables, mostly of statistics for the 1970s and early 1980s.

22 **The face of South America: an aerial traverse.**
John Lyon Rich. New York: American Geographical Society,
1942. 299p. 8 maps.

Despite the date of publication, this is still an outstanding vista of South American landscapes, including central and northern Chile (p. 163-208). Fifty-seven air photographs of these regions illustrate graphically the contrast between the fertile central valley and the northern desert, and there are some excellent pictures of nitrate establishments that were still working at the time.

23 **Chile land and society.**
George McCutchen McBride. New York: American Geographical
Society, 1936. 408p. bibliog. (American Geographical Society.
Research Series no. 19)

Although recent research on agrarian Chile has added to our knowledge of the subject, this classic description of the rural scene has not been entirely superseded and still repays reading. It is particularly valuable as a commentary on Chilean rural society at a time when the formerly dominant landowners were being challenged by new forces in politics and the economy, such as industrialists and bankers, and still stands as a basic study on the evolution of the Chilean *hacienda*, the great estate.

24 **When the earth trembles.**
Haroun Tazieff, translated from the French by Patrick O'Brian.
London: Hart-Davies, 1964. 228p. bibliog. 16 maps.

Chile is one of the most earthquake-prone countries in the world, given its narrow width, between the mountain chain of the Andes in the east and some of the world's deepest sea-trenches in the west. It has experienced some devastating shocks, for example that of 1906 which virtually destroyed Valparaiso, its chief port. The 'quake of May, 1960, which largely affected the south-central part of the country, cost an estimated 10,000 lives, and towns such as Valdivia, Puerto Montt and Castro were severely damaged. This survey of that event, by the noted French authority on such phenomena, is a graphic account which also includes comparative material on other earthquakes in Latin America and elsewhere, including the notorious Lisbon earthquake of 1755.

Regional

25 **Desert trails of Atacama.**
Isaiah Bowman. New York: American Geographical Society,
1924. 362p. 9 maps. (American Geographical Society. Special
Publication no. 5).

The result of three field expeditions to Chile's northern desert by a distinguished north American geographer, this detailed and well-illustrated account remains a classic description, despite the economic changes which have occurred in the region since it was written.

26 **Vanishing trails of Atacama.**
   William E. Rudolph.   New York: American Geographical Society, 1963. 86p. bibliog. 2 maps. (Research Series, no. 24).

An excellent study of the desert region, which might be considered as bringing the reader more up to date on its geography since the classic study of Isaiah Bowman (q.v.). Both, in fact, should be read together to measure the changes in the region over time.

27 **Arica: a desert frontier in transition.**
   J. Valerie Fifer.   *Geographical Journal*, vol. 130, part 4 (Dec. 1964), p. 507-18. 4 maps.

An excellent short article on Chile's northernmost town, a free port and the key transit point for Bolivian and Peruvian traffic to Chile.

28 **Chiloé et les chilotes: marginalité et dépendance en Patagonie chilienne – étude de géographie humaine.** (Chiloé and the Chilotes: marginality and dependence in Chilean Patagonia – a study in human geography.)
   Philippe Grenier.   Aix-en-Provence: Edisud, 1984. 592p. 32 maps. bibliog.

The French tradition of regional geography, of dissecting the parts to understand the whole, could not be better exemplified than in this detailed study of the large, and largely impoverished, Chilean island of Chiloé, which lies to the south of mainland Chile. It is a classic work, embellished with figures and photographs and a bibliography of over fifty pages.

29 **The Bío-Bío region of Chile in the later nineteenth century: a trade analysis.**
   John H. Whaley Jnr.   *Inter-American Economic Affairs*, vol. 29, no. 3 (winter 1975), p. 35-50.

A regional study which is interesting from the geographical, historical and economic points of view.

30 **Ocean surveyors in the Chilean fjords.**
   Peter Wadhams.   *Geographical Magazine*, vol. 44, no. 8 (May 1972), p. 563-67. map.

Stretching for some 1,600 km., between the town of Puerto Montt south to Cape Horn, Chile's fjord region is of great scenic attraction. This account is based on the visit made by the Canadian ship *Hudson* in 1970, and is a useful survey, with some illustrations.

31 **Mysterious volcanoes of the high Andes.**
    P. W. Francis. *Geographical Magazine*, vol. 42, no. 11
    (Aug. 1970), p. 795-803. 3 maps.
This article is the account of a geological expedition, by a team from Imperial
College, of the University of London, to study the pattern of volcanic activity in
the high Andes of north-eastern Chile. It is well illustrated.

32 **The Chilean cordillera central.**
    Evelio Echevarría. *Alpine Journal*, vol. 64, no. 299 (Nov. 1959),
    p. 228-36, and vol. 65, no. 300 (May 1960), p. 53-61. bibliog. maps.
An excellent description of the central part of the Chilean Andes, the backdrop to
Santiago and other cities in the central valley, which have ice-peaks ranging from
10,000 to 21,000 feet in height, in which part of the narrative is devoted to a
mountaineering expedition to climb three peaks of over 15,000 feet.

33 **Changing land occupance in the southern Chilean provinces of Aysén
    and Magallanes.**
    G. J. Butland. *Geographical Studies* (London: Birkbeck College),
    vol. 1, no. 1, 1954. p. 27-43. 7 maps.
The author, a geographer who spent some years in southern Chile, surveys the
changing landscape of the country's southernmost regions, which, though
comprising about one-third of the national territory, contain only about one-
fortieth of the population. Oil and sheep-farming are the basic economic activities
of this area.

34 **The human geography of southern Chile.**
    G. J. Butland. London: George Philip, 1957. 132p. 29 maps.
    bibliog. (Institute of British Geographers. Publication no. 24.)
Based on four years' residence in the world's southernmost city, Punta Arenas,
and on numerous field trips into Chilean Patagonia, Tierra del Fuego and
Magallanes, this is an excellent example of regional geography in an historical
setting. Butland surveys the physical landscape, provides a detailed account of the
historical evolution of settlement, and considers the region's economy and
problems at the time of writing. Though the latter part has been somewhat
superseded by the development of energy resources, this book remains the best
introduction to the region.

35 **The central tower of Paine.**
    C. J. S. Bonnington. *Alpine Journal*, vol. 68, no. 307 (Nov. 1963).
    p. 179-87.
Written by a well-known British mountaineer, this is a descriptive account of one
of Chile's most impressive mountain peaks, in the southern Andes of Patagonia,
which was climbed by the author. He embellishes his narrative with some graphic
photographs of the towers of the Paine group.

36 **Map-making on the Patagonian ice-cap.**
C. H. Agnew. *Geographical Magazine*, vol. 46, no. 12
(Sept. 1974), p. 709-13. map.

A British Joint Services expedition spent five months in Chile in 1972-73, concentrating on the glaciology of Chile's northernmost ice-field in the sparsely-populated region of Aysén. Their photographs revised the cartography of the area, and this account, with nine illustrations, is recommended reading for mountaineers and map-makers.

37 **Historia del estrecho de Magallanes.** (History of the Magellan
Straits.)
Mateo Martinic Beros.   Santiago: Editorial Andrés Bello, 1977.
261p. maps. bibliog.

The author, who lives in Punta Arenas, the world's southernmost town, is the leading authority on this region. This is a very useful geographical and historical account of the major route from the Atlantic to the Pacific before the opening of the Panama Canal in 1914.

38 **Tierra del Fuego: the fatal lodestone.**
Eric Shipton.   London: Charles Knight, 1973. 175p. map. (Latin
America Adventure Series).

A marvellous account by the leading British explorer of unknown Chile, especially the far south, which traces the history of its discovery by one who played a distinguished part in it.

39 **Islands beyond Cape Horn.**
Richard Hough. *Geographical Magazine*, (June 1975), p. 561-66.
map.

The author and his wife visited the Diego Ramírez group of islands, Chile's southernmost outpost north of Antarctica, and this is his account. Apart from those who man the weather station, the only inhabitants are penguins and falcons.

40 **La Antártica chilena.** (The Chilean Antarctic.)
Oscar Pinochet de la Barra.   Santiago: Editorial Andrés Bello,
1976. 4th ed. 210p.

First published in 1944, this pioneering work is still the basic book for Chilean geopoliticians and nationalists justifying Chile's claim to part of the Antarctic continent.

Maps and atlases

41   **Atlas cartográfico del reino de Chile. Siglos XVII-XIX.**
     (Cartographic atlas of the kingdom of Chile. Seventeenth to
     nineteenth centuries.)
     Santiago: Instituto Geográfico Militar, 1981. 266p.

This is a sumptuous production, for which a knowledge of Spanish is not entirely
necessary. It reproduces maps and drawings, for the centuries it spans, on Chilean
geography, town plans, etc. and is a beautiful book.

42   **Atlas de la república de Chile.** (Atlas of the republic of Chile.)
     Santiago: Ministerio de Defensa Nacional. Instituto Geográfico
     Militar, 1970. 244p.

While primarily consisting of topographical maps of Chile from north to south on
a scale of 1: 1,000,000, the atlas also has thematic maps on such topics as climate,
population, geology, etc. There is a gazetteer at the end. Altitude in the
topographic maps is indicated by tinting. There are also some excellent
photographs. The text is in Spanish, English and French. This work is
recommended.

43   **Atlas: Chile y sus nuevas provincias.** (Atlas: Chile and its new
     provinces.)
     Rudy Schmidt Walters, Patricio Valdés Sagrista.
     Santiago: Dirección de Fronteras y Límites del Estado, 1976. 32p.
     bibliog. maps.

As a measure of administrative reform, in the late 1960s, the historical Chilean
provinces were grouped into twelve regions. This is an atlas which reflects that
change, contains general descriptions of the twelve regions and may be
recommended to the non-specialist.

52 **Chile: its land and people. The history, natural features, development and industrial resources of a great South American republic.**
Francis J. G. Maitland.   London: Francis Griffiths, 1914. 293p. map.

A description of Chile on the eve of the First World War, which gives much useful information and contains a number of photographs evoking the period.

53 **2000 miles through Chile. The land of more or less.**
Earl Chapin May.   London, New York: Century, 1924. 462p. map.

The author travelled from the desert north of Chile to the far south and his observations, both serious and anecdotal, are an excellent evocation of the 1920s, as are the seventy-odd photographs.

54 **Chile.**
Erna Fergusson.   New York: Alfred A. Knopf, 1943. 341p. map.

The author, an American traveller, visited almost every part of Chile and her account provides a very interesting survey of the country and its people in the early 1940s.

55 **Chile through embassy windows: 1939-1953.**
Claude G. Bowers.   New York: Simon & Schuster, 1958. 375p.
Reprinted, Westport, Connecticutt: Greenwood, 1977.

The author served for fourteen years as ambassador of the United States in Chile, and this book is packed with information about his time there. Much of it is personal and anecdotal but there is also a good deal of comment on Chile during the Second World War and its aftermath, as well as acute observations on the Chile he knew. It is a valuable collection of reminiscences.

56 **The useless land: a winter in the Atacama desert.**
John Aarons, Claudio Vita-Finzi.   London: Hale, 1960. 191p. map.

In 1958, four Cambridge graduates in geography explored part of the northern half of the Atacama desert, one of the world's most barren regions. Twenty illustrations embellish the lively account of their adventures and their encounters with people of the region.

57 **Land of tempest: travels in Patagonia, 1958-62.**
Eric Shipton.   London: Hodder & Stoughton, 1963. 224p. 3 maps.

This is the author's account of four expeditions to southern Chile and Argentina, by the outstanding British explorer of the region. There are twenty-five evocative illustrations of ice-caps and glaciers and superb photographs. Several unnamed peaks were climbed by the author and his small team. The book also describes the author's meetings with Patagonian settlers. In many respects, the book is a compilation of research reports, by the author, in learned journals.

Exploration and Travel

58 **Crossing the north Patagonian ice-cap.**
Eric Shipton. *Alpine Journal*, vol. 309, no. 309 (Nov. 1964),
p. 183-90.
The veteran British explorer and mountaineer, Eric Shipton, traversed the San
Rafael galcier to Lago Colonia and the Río Colonia in November 1963. This is his
account of an expedition to one of Chile's least populated regions but one of great
scenic beauty. Unfortunately, there is no map.

59 **Cucumber sandwiches in the Andes.**
John Ure. London: Constable, 1973. 165p. bibliog. map.
This account was written by a British diplomat who, during his time in Santiago,
sought to retrace, though in the opposite direction, General San Martín's
celebrated crossing of the Andes in the wars for independence. The author
interweaves passages on Chilean history into this charmingly written account of
his journey on horseback.

60 **The Chilean way: travels in Chile.**
Nancy Phelan. London: Macmillan, 1973. 261p.
A quite well-written and sympathetic account of the author's travels in Chile in
the early 1970s.

61 **Elephant Island. An Antarctic expedition.**
Chris Furse. Shrewsbury, England: Anthony Nelson, 1979. 256p.
bibliog. 7 maps.
Elephant Island lies on the north-eastern rim of that part of the Antarctic
continent claimed by Chile. Together with its neighbours – Gibbs, O'Brien and
Clarence, names which reflect the contribution of British cartography to the
knowledge of that region – it was visited by the author in 1976-77 in his capacity
as leader of an expedition travelling by canoe to study various subjects such as
marine sciences, ornithology, geology, and so on. This report is well-produced,
with adequate bibliographies to the particular sections and excellent sketch-maps
and drawings by the author. This work makes an excellent scientific contribution
to Antarctic studies.

62 **The springs of enchantment. Climbing and exploration in Patagonia.**
John Earle. Sevenoaks, England: Hodder & Stoughton, 1981.
191p. 4 maps.
This book deals with two expeditions to southern Chile, mostly in the Chilean
part of the island of Tierra del Fuego, the first led by the distinguished British
climber and explorer, Eric Shipton, in 1963, the second, in 1979, when the author
was a cameraman for the BBC. They are very sympathetic accounts of the region
and its people and are well worth reading.

63 **Back to Cape Horn.**
Rosie Swale. London: Collins, 1986. 223p. 6 maps.
The author of this fascinating book is a British traveller and writer who, having

sailed round the world via Cape Horn in 1972-73, and crossed the Atlantic alone ten years later, set off in the middle of 1984 to ride on horseback from the Atacama desert to Cape Horn, a journey which took over 400 days. This account of her travels, travails and triumphs is well-written and repays reading, not only as an autobiographical adventure but also for its insights into the Chile which lies off the normal tourist track.

Travel guides

64 **The South American handbook.**
Edited by John Brooks with the assistance of Joyce Candy, Ben
Box. Bath, England: Trade & Travel Publications, 1987. 1344p.

This annual guide, now in its sixty-fourth year has long been recognized as the outstanding *vade-mecum* for the traveller in Latin America, and won the first ever Thomas Cook Best Travel Guide Award several years ago. It is quite outstandingly comprehensive, the section on Chile (p. 372-449), being eloquently descriptive of the entire country and containing all the relevant information the traveller may require.

65 **Michael's guide. Argentina, Chile, Paraguay and Uruguay.**
Michael Shichor.   Tel Aviv: Inbal Travel Information, 1987. 226p.
maps.

Though not as comprehensive as the *South American handbook*, this is still a useful guide on where to go and what to see. Over fifty pages (p. 130-87) are devoted to Chile. The book is also charmingly illustrated. More detail on specific cities and areas and practical advice on travel to and within Chile may be found in Alan Samagalski's *Chile & Easter Island* - a travel survival kit (274p.), published in Victoria, Australia and Berkeley, California in 1987 by Lonely Planet. This book also gives background information on Chilean history and society and is well illustrated.

66 **Backpacking in Chile and Argentina, plus the Falkland islands.**
Hilary Bradt, John Pilkington.   Boston, Massachusetts; Chalfont
St. Peter, England: Bradt Enterprises, 1980. 128p. bibliog. maps.

A very straightforward and informative hitch-hikers' guide, which is illustrated and contains much practical advice on walking in these countries.

15

Flora and Fauna

67 **South America and Central Ameria: a natural history.**
Jean Dorst. London: Hamish Hamilton, 1967. 298p. (The
Continents We Live On).

This lavishly illustrated survey of Latin American nature has sections on Chile
covering, in particular, the Atacama desert, Patagonia, Tierra del Fuego and
Antarctica.

68 **Biogeography and ecology in South America.**
Edited by E. J. Fittkau, J. Illies, H. Klinge, G. H. Schwabe,
H. Sioli. The Hague: Dr. W. Junk, N. V., 1969. 946p. bibliog.
maps. (Monographiae Biologicae vol. 18-19).

A comprehensive collection of essays, in English and German, on the fauna and
insects of the sub-continent in their various habitats. It covers fossils, mammals,
coleoptera, birds, fresh-water fish, arachnidae, mammals, molluscs, and so on.
This exhaustive survey includes Chile, but the treatment is thematic rather than
geographical.

69 **Sinopsis de la flora chilena. Claves para su identificación de familias
y géneros.** (Synopsis of Chilean flora. Keys for the identification of
families and species.)
Carlos Muñoz Pizarro. Santiago: Ediciones de la Universidad de
Chile, 1966. 2nd ed. 500p.

With more than 240 original illustrations by E. Sierra Rafols and F. Sudsuki, this
splendid book gives an ample description of families and species of Chilean flora
in a systematic form. It also has good indexes.

70   **Medicina tradicional chilena.** (Traditional Chilean medicine.)
     Marco Montés, Tatiana Wilkomirsky.   Concepción: Editorial de la
     Universidad de Concepción, 1985. 205p.
Partly based on various theses, this is a guide to medicinal plants, their properties
and their chemical components.

71   **El árbol urbano en Chile.** (The urban tree in Chile.)
     Adriana Hoffmann.   Santiago: Ediciones Fundación Claudio Gay,
     1983. 225p.
As in other areas of Latin America, where urbanization has proceeded apace in
the past fifty years, Chilean cities, and notably the capital, Santiago, have large
numbers of parks and gardens with a wide variety of trees and shrubs. This
beautifully illustrated book brings that fact to life, and includes a useful glossary
and index to the different species. It is a superbly produced volume.

72   **Flora of Tierra del Fuego.**
     David M. Moore.   Oswestry, England; St. Louis, Missouri: Missouri
     Botanical Gardens, 1983. 396p. bibliog.
An extraordinarily detailed account of the island's flora, in which each species is
described in detail, with line-drawings, location maps, and some colour photos. A
general introduction to the island is followed by a history of botanical exploration,
supplemented at the end of the book by a chronological summary of plant
collectors from 1690 to 1980. A beautiful book and one which appeals not only to
botanists.

73   **Flores silvestres de Chile.** (Wild flowers of Chile.)
     Carlos Muñoz Pizarro.   Santiago: Ediciones de la Universidad de
     Chile, 1966. 245p.
This is a very attractive book with fifty-one beautiful original paintings, in colour.
The entries are by family and species and the descriptions of the flowers are
comprehensive.

74   **The oceanic birds of South America.**
     Robert Cushman Murphy.   New York: American Museum of
     Natural History, 1936. 2 vols. bibliog.
A standard reference work, which covers the species of oceanic birds of Chile,
though the arrangement is not by geographical region.

75   **The birds of Chile and adjacent regions of Argentina, Bolivia and
     Peru.**
     A. W. Johnson, colour plates by J. D. Goodall.   Buenos Aires:
     Platt Establecimientos Gráficos, S. A., 1965. 397p. bibliog. map.
A comprehensive description with details of the locations of species and families,
which is embellished with 100 painted colour illustrations and some black-and-
white photographs.

76 **Geographical ecology of small mammals in the northern Chilean arid zone.**
Peter L. Meserve, William E. Glanz. *Journal of Biogeography*, vol. 2, no. 2. (June 1978), p. 135-48. map.

This is the report of a study of small mammal communities at nine localities on the north Chilean coast. The work was carried out in 1973-74, and each locality was sampled twice. The major conclusion was that the numbers of total species decreased from south to north.

Archaeology

77 **Prehistoria de Chile.** (Prehistory of Chile.)
Greta Mostny. Santiago: Editorial Universitaria, 1971. 3rd ed.
185p.

This is the latest revised edition of a well-known short introduction to Chilean
history, from the palaeoindian period to the Spanish conquest.

78 **An introduction to American archaeology. Vol. 2. South America.**
Gordon R. Willey. Englewood Cliffs, New Jersey: Prentice-Hall,
1971. 559p. bibliog. 22 maps.

Though a large general work on the archaeology of the sub-continent, this survey,
by a *doyen* of American archaeology, contains recondite material on Chile, with
references to pre-hispanic cultures ranging from the Atacameño and the Diaguita
in the north to the Ona and Yahgan in the far south, and many illustrations.

79 **Palaeoindio y arcaico en Chile: diversidad, secuencia y procesos.**
(The palaeoindian and archaic in Chile: diversity, sequence and
process.)
Lautaro Núñez Atencio. Mexico City: Instituto Nacional de
Antropología e Historia, 1983. 205p. bibliog. map. (Serie
Monografías, no. 3).

This is a valuable review by the leading authority on the palaeoindian and archaic
phases of Chilean cultures, covering the desert and semi-desert north, the central
valley and the semi-desert south, including carbon dates to late 1980. A work
which is primarily for the archaeologist, but is also an important contribution to
the existing evidence of early man in Chile.

19

80   **Actas.** (Proceedings.)
Eighth Chilean Congress of Archaeology. Sociedad Chilena de
Arqueología, Universidad Austral de Chile, 1979.   Valdivia:
Ediciones Kultrun, 1982. 324p. bibliog. maps.

Though Chile does not possess such impressive archaeological monuments as
other Latin American countries such as Mexico, Peru and Bolivia, it does have an
important range of sites throughout its territory, from the desert north to the far
south, and a number of distinguished archaeologists. This collection of papers,
given at the eighth congress of archaeology in 1979, covers such diverse subjects
as the *chullpas* (funerary monuments) at Likán in the north, an Inca *tambo*
(staging-post) at Chungara, near Arica, the late pre-Inca sites and artefacts
between the rivers Aconcagua and Cachapoal in the central valley, and the much
earlier carbon-dated fishing and hunting sites of the prehistoric periods on the
southern coast and Magallanes. The time-scale is from the eighth mil ennium BP
to the fifteenth century AD.

81   **Contributions to the archaeology of the river Loa region.**
Stig Rydén.   Gothenburg, Sweden: Elanders Boktryckeri
Aktiebolag, 1944. 250p. bibliog.

This general description of the Loa valley in the northern region of the Chilean
Atacama desert deals with the pre-hispanic cultures. It considers a wide range of
archaeological material, such as burials, artefacts, pottery, rock paintings and
textiles, at various sites such as Lazana, Chiu-chiu and Tiara, some of the earliest
Spanish colonial settlements in Chile which also have a long, pre-Inca past.

82   **Prehistoric trails of Atacama: archaeology of northern Chile.**
Edited by Clement W. Meighan, D. L. True.   Los Angeles:
Institute of Archaeology, University of California, 1980. 228p.
bibliog. (Monumenta Archaeológica, 0363-7565;7).

Little work in Chilean archaeology is published in English and this is definitely the
most informative study of the north coast, based on joint Chilean-American
research in the 1970s. It presents a new chronology, based on C14 dating, and
specialized reports on artefacts, fish and animal remains, plant remains and fossil
excrement.

83   **Paleo-indian and archaic cultural periods in the arid and semiarid
regions of northern Chile.**
Lautaro Núñez.   In: *Advances in world archaeology*. Edited by
Fred Wendorf, Angela Close, New York: Academic Press, 1983.
vol. 2, p. 161-203. bibliog.

The author, one of Chile's outstanding archaeologists, and a particular authority
on the northern desert regions, presents here a review of sites, artefacts, remains
and other material, to show the transition from subsistence based on wild plants
and animals to that using domestic ones. It is based on his own fieldwork and C14
dating.

84 **Fishermen, mummies and balsa rafts on the coast of northern Chile.**
Bente Bittmann. *El Dorado*. Greeley, Colorado: Museum of
Anthropology, vol. 3, no. 3 (1978), p. 60-103. bibliog.
The author, who is a leading archaeologist working in northern Chile, presents
here an argument that, possibly, cultural groups on Chile's coast were influenced
by groups further north, from early formative times. The article is illustrated.

85 **Catalogue of fossil hominids. Part 3, the Americas, Asia, Australia.**
Edited by Kenneth Page Oakley, Bernard Grant Campbell.
London: British Museum of Natural History, 1975. bibliog. 9 maps.
228p.
One of three catalogues listing fossil discoveries throughout the world, including
Chile. Details are given of location, age, flora and fauna, related artefacts,
physical measurements, and so on.

86 **The first Americans: origins, affinities and adaptations.**
Edited by William S. Laughlin, Albert B. Harper. New York:
G. Fischer, 1979. 340p. bibliog.
Fifteen chapters cover the origins and evolution of the earliest peoples in the New
World, as well as the latest theories on their ancestry, provenance and the timing
of the first migrations. Before the Spaniards, Chile had a range of Indian peoples,
from the Atacama desert to Tierra del Fuego.

87 **Arte rupestre chileno.** (Chilean rock art.)
Greta Mostny, Hans Niemeyer Fernández. Santiago: Ministerio de
Educación, Departmento de Exptensión Cultural, [n.d.]. 150p.
bibliog. maps. (Serie El Patrimonio Cultural Chileno. Colección
Historia Del Arte Chileno).
An introduction to Chilean rock-art for the non-specialist, covering the location,
motifs, technique and so on of nine local styles and comparing the different
representations of animals, humans, geometric figures, with comments on
chronology. The non-Spanish reader will, at least, delight in the splendid colour
illustrations.

88 **The eighth land: the Polynesian discovery and settlement of Easter
Island.**
Thomas S. Barthel, translated from the German by Annaliese
Martin. Honolulu: University Press of Hawaii, 1978. 372p.
bibliog.
The author collected a lot of ethnohistorical material, including oral traditions, on
Easter Island, in the late 1950s, and this book is his definitive account. Chile
annexed the island in 1888.

89   **Archaeology of Easter Island.**
      Edited by Thor Heyerdahl, Edwin N. Feardon, Jr.   London: Allen
      & Unwin, 1962. p. 559. maps. bibliog. (Norwegian Archaeological
      Expedition to Easter Island and the East Pacific Report, vol. 1).

This, the most comprehensive survey of the archaeology of Chile's major Pacific
possession, is lavishly illustrated with 96 plates and 138 figures. Heyerdahl's
conviction that the aboriginal South Americans peopled Polynesia is mooted in
this very scholarly and detailed study.

Anthropology

90   **Handbook of South American Indians.**
Edited by Julian H. Steward.   New York: Cooper Square, 1963.
7 vols. bibliog.

In this facsimile reproduction of the original publication (1946-59), volume two on the Andean civilizations includes articles on aboriginal Chilean peoples, ranging from the Diaguita in the north to the Ona of Tierra del Fuego in the far south. A classic work, first published as Bulletin 143 of the Smithsonian Institution, Bureau of American Ethnology, it is still worth consulting, despite its date.

91   **Native peoples of South America.**
Julian H. Steward, Louis C. Faron.   New York, Toronto, London: McGraw Hill, 1959. 479p. bibliog.

A classic work by two distinguished North American anthropologists, which makes particular reference to the different types of South American native cultures including Chile and their relationships with their European conquerors.

92   **The Mapuche Indians of Chile.**
Louis C. Faron.   New York: Holt, Rinehart & Winston, 1968.
111p.

Based on fieldwork, this is an excellent account of the history and present situation of the major aboriginal people of Chile. The Mapuche resisted European conquest until the last quarter of the nineteenth century. They are now confined largely to reservations in the southern province of Cautín. This sympathetic portrayal is written in concise, non-technical language.

Anthropology

93 **Memorias de un cacique mapuche.** (Memoirs of a Mapuche chief.)
Pascual Coña. Santiago: Instituto de Capacitación e Investigación
en Reforma Agraria (Institute for Training and Research in
Agrarian Reform), 1973. 464p.

The author of this quite remarkable autobiography was a pure-blooded Mapuche
Indian of southern Chile, who died, over eighty years of age, in 1930. The first
edition appeared in the same year and this facsimile reproduction, with both the
Mapuche text and Spanish translation, together with an article on the Mapuche
from the *Revista Chilena de Historia y Geografía* (The Chilean Journal of History
and Geography) by a German missionary of last century who lived among them,
is a meritorious production. It is a detailed account of Chile's most significant
Indian race by a native who was born before the Mapuche lost their
independence.

94 **Mapuche social structure: institutional reintegration in a patrilineal
society of central Chile.**
Louis C. Faron. Urbana, Illinois: University of Illinois Press,
1961. 247p. bibliog. map. (Illinois Studies in Anthropology, no. 1).

The leading non-Spanish authority on the Mapuche, Chile's largest Indian tribe,
presents here a professional account of their life and activities on their
reservations in south-central Chile.

95 **Hawks of the sun. Mapuche morality and its ritual attributes.**
Louis C. Faron. Pittsburgh: University of Pittsburgh Press, 1964.
220p. bibliog.

A professional piece of anthropological writing which was produced by the
leading English-speaking authority on the Mapuche Indians of Chile. The author
discusses the Mapuche social structure in the context of their religious beliefs and
conduct.

96 **Life on a half-share: mechanisms of social recruitment among the
Mapuche of southern Chile.**
Milan Stuchlik. New York: St. Martin's, 1976. 222p. bibliog.

Produced on the basis of fieldwork in three Mapuche communities in the province
of Cautín in 1968-70, this is very much a work for specialists in anthropology. It is
a detailed and well-documented account of how individuals in Mapuche society
recruit helpers in different situations. It does not, nor was it intended to, deal
with the broader issue of the relationship between this large native race of Latin
America and the Chilean successors to the Spaniards who failed to conquer them,
an issue that might have been of more interest to the layman. However, it makes
a useful anthropological contribution.

97 **The national integration of Mapuche ethnical minority in Chile.**
Staffan Berglund, translated from the Swedish by Bernard
Wolves. Stockholm: Almqvist & Wiksell International, 1977.
228p. maps. bibliog.

This is almost as much a political as an anthropological study. It is a study of

24

Chile's largest aboriginal minority people, based on fieldwork carried out in 1972-73. It is, in part, an interesting account of the attitudes to, and policies for, this neglected segment of Chilean society by the socialist government of Salvador Allende.

98 Araucanian child life and its cultural background.

M. Iñez Hilger. Washington, DC: Smithsonian Institution, 1957. 439p. bibliog. map. (Smithsonian Misc. Collections, no. 133).

An exhaustive study, which is the product of fieldwork among the Araucanians (or Mapuche) in both Chile and Argentina in the late 1940s and early 1950s. Despite the date of publication, much of the data on Indian life is still relevant, and the bibliography is extensive. This remains a very important anthropological study.

99 Agrarian reform in Chile and its impact on Araucanian Indian communities.

Bernardo Berdichewsky. In: *Anthropology and social change in rural areas*. Edited by Bernardo Berdichewsky. The Hague, Paris, New York: Mouton, 1979, p. 433–60. (World Anthropology Series).

A short but useful survey, written against the historical background of the reservation system applied to Chile's largest native tribe since the nineteenth century. The author summarizes the effects on land tenure of the agrarian reforms of the Frei government (1964-70) and beyond.

100 Drama and power in a hunting society: the Selk'nam of Tierra del Fuego.

Anne Chapman. Cambridge: Cambridge University Press, 1982. 201p. bibliog.

The Selk'nam were the southernmost hunting tribe in the world, occupying parts of both the Chilean and Argentine portions of the island of Tierra del Fuego. This is an outstanding piece of anthropological research, based on field-trips and oral evidence provided by the very few members of the tribe who have survived to the 1980s. It is a detailed reconstruction of their life and culture and, in a sense, a memorial to the Selk'nam, who were, like other Amerindians, victims of 'civilization'.

History

General

101 Chile: the legacy of hispanic capitalism.
Brian Loveman.   New York: Oxford University Press, 1979. 429p.
bibliog.

The best single-volume history of Chile in English to date. Based essentially upon secondary sources, but without footnotes, the book has an outstanding bibliographical section, indicating the author's familiarity with his field. An important introductory text, tracing Chilean history from the Spanish conquest in the 1540s to the fall of President Allende in 1973.

102 Resumen de la historia de Chile, 1535-1925. (Summary of the
history of Chile, 1535-1925.)
Francisco Antonio Encina, Leopoldo Castedo.   Santiago: Empresa
Editora Zig-Zag, 1954-82. 4 vols. maps.

The twenty-volume history of Chile from 1535 to 1891, by Francisco Antonio Encina, which appeared in the early 1950s, is undoubtedly the longest and most detailed narrative to be written this century. Subsequently, in a collaborative work between Encina and a distinguished compatriot and historian, Leopoldo Castedo, the twenty volumes were condensed into three, replete, unlike the original, with illustrations, maps, statistical tables and so on. They lacked, however, as did the original text, references. Nearly thirty years later, Castedo himself took the story from 1891 to 1925, in a sumptuously-produced volume of nearly 1,000 pages, beautifully illustrated and with full references. Encina was a controversial historian but his work cannot be ignored. The volume by Castedo is a major contribution to twentieth-century Chilean history for those who have Spanish.

103 **Francisco Encina and revisionism in Chilean history.**
Charles C. Griffin. *Hispanic American Historical Review*, vol. 37, no. 1 (Feb. 1957), p. 1-28.
Encina's twenty-volume *History of Chile*, from the earliest times to the civil war of 1891, is an enormously detailed account which has been the subject of much controversy, partly because of the author's unwillingness to cite his sources and also as a result of his nationalistic and racial attitudes. This article, by a distinguished American historian of Latin America, is a trenchant and important critique.

104 **The civil wars in Chile (or the bourgeois revolutions that never were).**
Maurice Zeitlin. Princeton, New Jersey: Princeton University Press, 1984. 265p. bibliog.
A controversial interpretation, written from a left-wing sociological standpoint, and based, essentially, on secondary sources, of the 'revolutions' of 1851, 1859 and 1891. The author seeks to prove that the three civil conflicts sprang largely from clashes of economic interest within the Chilean ruling class.

105 **Capitalism and underdevelopment in Latin America: historical studies of Chile and Brazil.**
André Gunder Frank. New York: Monthly Review, 1969. rev. ed. 344p. bibliog.
As a founding father of the 'dependency school' on Latin American development, the author wrote this book to prove the thesis that underdevelopment in Latin America is the result of external capitalist exploitation. Based entirely on selected secondary sources, its value to the historian is limited, but the book is important because of its theoretical implications and the impact it made on opinion in various disciplines.

106 **Chilean rural society from the Spanish conquest to 1930.**
Arnold J. Bauer. Cambridge: Cambridge University Press, 1975. 265p. bibliog. (Cambridge Latin American Studies, no. 21).
Developed, largely, from the author's doctoral dissertation, this detailed study of the Chilean landed aristocracy since the Spanish conquest is, so far, the definitive work on the subject. It is essential reading for an understanding of Chilean history, given the aristocracy's dominant positon in Chilean society for almost three centuries. Thoroughly researched and annotated, it is a model monograph.

107 **The military in Chilean history: essays on civil-military relations, 1810-1973.**
Frederick M. Nunn. Albuquerque, New Mexico: University of New Mexico Press, 1976. 343p.
The author is the leading authority, in the English-speaking world, on the military in Chile, one of the very few Latin American countries which, certainly until the coup of 1973, was thought to have established a constitutional and democratic

régime in which the armed forces were clearly subordinate to the civil power. Having studied both Chile and its institutions at length, Professor Nunn provides, in this book, something of a revision of that view, and gives new insight into the relationship between civilian government and the armed forces over time. Based on a wide variety of sources, this is a challenging study of an important subject, which helps to elucidate much of Chile's contemporary history against the background of the country's past.

108   **Chile from independence to the War of the Pacific.**
      Simon Collier.   In: *Cambridge History of Latin America*, vol. 3.
      Edited by Leslie Bethell. Cambridge: Cambridge University Press,
      1985, p. 583-613. map. bibliog.

This essay offers a succinct summary of the period by the leading British authority and gives an excellent introduction to the subject.

109   **Chile from the War of the Pacific to the world depression, 1880-1930.**
      Harold Blakemore.   In: *Cambridge History of Latin America*,
      vol. 4. Edited by Leslie Bethell. Cambridge: Cambridge
      University Press, 1986, p. 449-551. map. bibliog.

A short introduction to the period, which is based, in part, on original material.

110   **Estructura social de Chile. Estudio, selección de textos y bibliografía.** (Social structure of Chile. Study, selection of texts and bibliography.)
      Edited by Hernán Godoy.   Santiago: Editorial Universitaria,
      1971. 632p. bibliog.

Despite its title, this is a most valuable tool for historians. It consists of carefully selected extracts from a wide variety of sources on aspects of Chilean society, economy and politics, from the colonial period to the present day. It is an outstanding 'source' book, with an extensive bibliography.

111   **Aspects of class relations in Chile, 1850-1960.**
      Fredrick B. Pike.   *Hispanic American Historical Review*, vol. 43,
      no. 1. (Feb. 1963), p. 14-33.

An important article highlighting the continuity in Chilean history of the sharp social cleavage in society, and the continuing disdain of the upper classes for the lower.

112   **From colonialism to dependence: an introduction to Chile's economic history.**
      Stefan de Vylder.   Stockholm: Swedish International
      Development Authority, 1974. 72p. bibliog. (Development
      Studies, 1974:3)

The book provides a brief but very useful 'overview' of Chilean economic development down to 1970. The author argues that, from colonial times to the present, Chile's economy has suffered from structural defects which have never really been corrected, which has led to dependence on outside factors, beyond Chile's control.

113 **Robinson Crusoe's island. A history of the Juan Fernández Islands.**
Ralph Lee Woodward Jr. Chapel Hill, North Carolina: University of North Carolina Press, 1969. 267p. bibliog. 3 maps.

Indisputably the most useful history of the Islands in English, covering the period from their discovery in 1574, to 1966, not long after the author visited them. It is a detailed account, based essentially on secondary sources. This excellent book has not commanded much interest, but repays attention.

Colonial (1541-1810)

114 **Pedro de Valdivia. Conquistador of Chile.**
Ida W. Vernon. Austin, Texas: University of Texas Press, 1946. 193p. (Latin American Studies, no. 3). Reprinted, New York: Greenwood, 1969.

Valdivia (1502?-53) is to Chile what Cortés is to Mexico and Pizarro to Peru, that is, the founder of the Spanish colony. Between 1541, when he established Santiago, and his death at the hands of the Araucanian Indians of south-central Chile, he promoted the Spanish colonization of Chile. This biography is a solid work, though its prose does not quite match Don Pedro's exploits.

115 **The conqueror's lady, Inés Suárez.**
Stella Burke May. New York: Farrar & Rinehart, 1930. 331p. bibliog.

A somewhat romantic, though well-written, biography of the remarkable mistress of Pedro de Valdivia, conqueror of Chile, who took part in his exploits, before marrying one of his men, Rodrigo de Quiroga, subsequently governor of Chile. She lived from 1512 to 1580.

116 **The conquest of Chile.**
H. R. S. Pocock. New York: Stein & Day, 1967. 256p.

This is a very well-written account, based on contemporary chronicles and secondary literature, of the conquest of Chile by Pedro de Valdivia, covering the period up to his death in 1554. Written by an amateur historian, long resident in Chile, it is a detailed and lively narrative.

117 **The black experience in Chile.**
William F. Sater. In: *Slavery and race relations in Latin America.*
Edited by Robert Brent Toplin. Westport,
Connecticut: Greenwood, 1974, p. 13-50. map.

One of the few works in English to consider negro slavery in Chile, not as significant as elsewhere in the Spanish colonial empire. This is a very useful survey, based on a wide range of sources, of one aspect of race relations in the country's history.

118 **Spanish policy in colonial Chile: The struggle for social justice, 1535-1700.**
Eugene Korth, SJ. Stanford, California: Stanford University Press, 1968. map.

Though emphasizing the role of the Society of Jesus in the colonial evolution of Chile, this book offers a very good interpretation of the Spanish conquest and its impact, not least on the aboriginal population. Its value is enhanced by the comparative paucity of works in English on the colonial period.

119 **Frontier warfare in colonial Chile.**
Louis de Armond. *Pacific Historical Review*, vol. 23 (1954), p. 125-132.

This article offers one of the very few accounts in English of the relationship, during the colonial period, between the Spanish conquerors and the aboriginal Araucanian Indians of Chile. It is highly recommended.

120 **Urban social stratification in colonial Chile.**
Mario Góngora. *Hispanic American Historical Review*, vol. 55 (1975), p. 421-48.

Though quite short, this essay by an outstanding Chilean authority on the colonial period is an excellent portrait of the different social groups in Santiago and other cities in colonial Chile.

121 **Baroque tales of Chile.**
Henry Lyon Young. Ilfracombe, England: Arthur H. Stockwell, 1963. 207p.

Some chapters in this book are semi-fictional, but two, *The Virgin of Andacollo* and *La Quintrala*, evoke important phenomena of the colonial period. Andacollo, in northern Chile, celebrates, on 25th and 26th of December, a picturesque religious festival in honour of the Virgin of the Rosary of Andacollo, with pre-Spanish ritual dances. Legend claims that the Virgin appeared before an Indian named Collo and directed him to a gold mine. La Quintrala was a notorious woman of the colonial era.

122 **Byron of the *Wager*.**
Peter Shankland. London: William Collins, 1975. 288p. 2 maps.

John Byron, less well-known than his future grandson, the poet, was a midshipman on the *Wager* which, in 1740, formed part of a British squadron under Captain George Anson sent to attack Spanish settlements in the Pacific. Having rounded Cape Horn, however, the ship was wrecked on the island of Tierra del Fuego. Byron's journals recount the incredible story of what subsequently happened to the crew, some of whom, including Byron, journeyed from the far south to central Chile, and eventually back to England. This is a graphic narrative, based on original material, containing much interesting information on Chile at that time, notably on the Araucanian Indians.

123 **Reform and politics in Bourbon Chile, 1755-1796.**
Jacques A. Barbier. Ottawa: University of Ottawa Press, 1980.
218p. bibliog. (Cahiers d'Histoire, no. 10).

This well-researched monograph makes a most important contribution to the history of Chile in the late colonial period, emphasizing politics and government and social structure. The author, correctly, concentrates on Santiago, capital of the kingdom of Chile under Spanish imperial control, and assesses, in particular, the impact of the Bourbon reforms on Chile, which were the prelude to Chilean independence.

Independence (1810-33)

124 **Ideas and politics of Chilean independence, 1808-1833.**
Simon Collier. Cambridge: Cambridge University Press, 1967.
386p. bibliog. (Cambridge Latin American Studies, no. 1).

This is, without doubt, the authoritative history in English of the Chilean independence movement from Spain and its aftermath. Based on extensive archival research, primarily in Chilean and British repositories, it is a detailed account of a complicated period, describing its leading characters and their ideas. It is a quite indispensable book in Chilean historiography.

125 **Bernardo O'Higgins and the independence of Chile.**
Stephen Clissold. London: Rupert Hart-Davis, 1968. 254p. 4
maps.

The author of this book wrote a large number of books on Latin American historical subjects, derived, in part, from his experiences as a British public servant in various locations, including Chile. Although the literature on Chile's greatest national hero is enormous, most of it is in Spanish. This biography is an excellent account, based on the author's knowledge of the literature, aimed at the inquisitive English-speaking public. It can be highly recommended to the non-specialist as an accurate and literate study of a key figure in Chilean history.

126 **Kinship politics in the Chilean independence movement.**
Mary Lowenthal Felstiner. *Hispanic American Historical Review*,
vol. 56, no. 1 (Feb. 1976), p. 58-80.

An interesting and heavily-researched study of a key Chilean family, during the
independence period. The history of the Larraín clan can be traced from the
colonial period to the present day: it shows clearly the significance of family ties in
Chilean history, this being one of the country's most enduring characteristics.

127 **Rebel captain. The life and exploits of admiral Lord Cochrane,
tenth Earl of Dundonald.**
Frank Knight. London: MacDonald, 1968. 172p.

A biography, for the younger reader, of the remarkable seaman and adventurer
who, in effect, founded the Chilean navy during the wars of independence from
Spain.

128 **The sea wolf. The life of Admiral Cochrane.**
Ian Grimble. London: Blond & Briggs, 1978. 399p. bibliog.

An excellent biography of the great British seaman, though it is, perhaps, too
charitable to his character. His role in the Chilean struggle for independence is
conveyed effectively and there are interesting comments on his frequently
antagonistic contemporaries.

129 **The manning of the Chilean navy in the war of independence, 1818-
1823.**
David J. Cubitt. *Mariner's Mirror*, vol. 63, no. 2 (May 1977),
p. 115-27. bibliog.

The author has made an original piece of research into Chilean naval history. He
gives the number and the national origin of the mariners (most of them Chilean)
and considers the process of recruitment. The article is a useful contribution to
the history of the independence period.

130 **Cochrane y la independencia del Pacífico.** (Cochrane and the
independence of the Pacific.)
Alamiro de Avila Martel. Santiago: Editorial Universitaria, 1976.
306p.

An excellent study, based on primary as well as secondary sources, which
considers the naval warfare during the war of independence, and the role of
Thomas Cochrane, the founder of the Chilean navy. His critics, including the
Argentine 'liberator', General José de San Martín, are soundly rebutted.

131 **The Irisarri loan.**
Claudio Véliz. *Boletín de Estudios Latinoamericanos y del
Caribe*, no. 23 (Dec. 1977), p. 3-20.

In 1822, Antonio José Irisarri, acting as agent for the government of Bernardo
O'Higgins, raised the first Chilean state loan abroad. This carefully researched
article considers that transaction and decides, correctly, that not only was the loan

unnecessary but that London bankers profited from it, while its adverse effects in Chile were a contributory factor in the fall of O'Higgins himself. An excellent research article on the early finances of the infant republic.

132   **The introduction of classical economics into Chile.**
     Robert M. Will.   *Hispanic American Historical Review*, vol. 44,
     no. 1 (Feb. 1964), p. 1-21.
An important analysis of Chilean governmental policy in the aftermath of independence. The author contradicts previous views and cogently asserts that the fathers of independence did not make such a radical break with the protectionist policies of the empire as has been supposed.

133   **The early constitutions of Chile.**
     Paul Vanorden Shaw.   Columbia: Columbia University Press,
     1930. 181p. bibliog.
A survey of the constitutions of Chile in the decade or so after independence, which includes that of 1833 which lasted, with amendments, until 1925. The author has a rather pedestrian style but his study illustrates the problems of the infant republic in creating a workable constitutional form.

134   **Diego Portales: interpretative essays on the man and times.**
     Jay Kinsbruner.   The Hague: Martinus Nijhoff, 1967. 102p.
The author puts forward a 'revisionist' view, in five essays, of the life and work of Portales, who is generally regarded as the key figure in the establishment of the constitutional republic of Chile after the turbulence of independence and its aftermath. He challenges the traditional view which sees Portales as the guiding hand of the constitution of 1833, and the landed aristocracy as its patrons. He emphasizes his view that Portales was a political pragmatist and also an ignoramus on economics. The work is, perhaps, too short for a convincing elaboration of these ideas but is, nonetheless, challenging.

From independence to the War of the Pacific (1833-79)

135   **The impact of market agriculture on family and household structure in nineteenth-century Chile.**
     Ann Hagerman Johnson.   *Hispanic American Historical Review*,
     vol. 58, no. 4 (Nov. 1978), p. 625-48.
A pioneering analysis in Chilean social history, showing how traditional household structures and family relationships in a selected rural area in the Chilean central valley were affected by economic change.

136 **Before the gold fleets: trade and relations between Chile and Australia, 1830-1848.**
Thomas M. Bader. *Journal of Latin American Studies*, vol. 6, part 1 (May 1974), p. 35-58.

An interesting study of a much neglected topic, considering, as the title indicates, the geopolitical advantages to both Chile and Australia of trading relationships between them. The author concentrates on the shipment of Chilean agrarian produce to Australia which decreased as the latter achieved greater self-sufficiency.

137 **Economic policy and growth in Chile from independence to the War of the Pacific.**
Luis Ortega. In: *Latin America: economic imperialism and the state*. Edited by Christopher Abel, Colin M. Lewis. London; Dover, New Hampshire: Athlone, 1985, p. 146-71. (University of London Institute of Latin American Studies Monographs, 13).

This gives an important and well-researched 'overview' of the evolution of the Chilean economy and of government policies towards economic development in the period covered.

138 **Before the nitrate era: British commission houses and the Chilean economy, 1851-80.**
John Mayo. *Journal of Latin American Studies*, vol. 11, part 2 (Nov. 1979), p. 283-302.

A most important and heavily researched article on the role of British traders in the development of the Chilean economy in this period. Using material from company records, the author explains the very close economic relationship between Britain and Chile, emphasizing the key role of the British in integrating Chile into the world market, whilst, at the same time, inhibiting the growth of Chilean industry.

139 **British merchants and Chilean development, 1851-1886.**
John Mayo. Boulder, Colorado: Westview, 1987. 250p. bibliog. (Dellplain Latin American Studies, no. 22).

Based on the author's Oxford doctoral dissertation, this well written and researched study is a major contribution to the history of the British role in Chilean development, which uses the archives of British companies operating in Chile as a major source. It may be highly recommended.

140 **Merchants and bankers: British direct and portfolio investment in Chile during the nineteenth century.**
Manuel A. Fernández. *Ibero-Amerikanische Archiv*, nueva epoca, año 9, cuaderno 3/4, 1983. p. 349-79.

A detailed study, with statistical data, of British investment in Chile, which has been written largely from a 'dependency' standpoint. While recognizing the vital role played by British capital in Chilean development, the author argues that the close relationship between British capitalists and the Chilean upper class was inimical to the lower classes in Chile.

141 William Wheelwright and early steam navigation in the Pacific.
Roland E. Duncan. *The Americas*, vol. 32, no. 2 (Oct. 1975), p. 257-81.

In a splendid essay in entrepreneurial history, the author studies the man who was the force behind the Liverpool-based Pacific Steam Navigation Company despite being himself a citizen of the United States. The company was the first to establish a steam-ship connection between Europe and Chile.

142 Chilean coal and British steamers: the origin of a South American industry.
Roland E. Duncan. *Mariner's Mirror*, vol. 61, no. 3, 1975. p. 271-81.

An interesting short essay which looks at the role of William Wheelwright, and that of British steamships, in the development of the Chilean coal industry.

143 The first four decades of the Chilean coal mining industry.
Luis Ortega. *Journal of Latin American Studies*, vol. 14, part 1, (May 1982), p. 1-32.

Very little has been written in English on this topic, and this thoroughly researched article, therefore, fills a conspicuous gap. The author also provides a number of relevant statistical tables in his convincing account of the growth of the Chilean coal mining industry, a mirror of the beginnings of national industrial enterprise. It is an exemplary study.

144 Water for Valparaiso: a case of entrepreneurial frustration.
Jay Kinsbruner. *Journal of Inter-American Studies*, vol. 10, no. 4 (Oct. 1968), p. 653-61.

This is a short but interesting article on the frustrated attempts of William Wheelwright, the American entrepreneur, to provide Valparaiso with a modern system of water supply.

145 Pioneer telegraphy in Chile, 1852-1876.
J. J. Johnson. Stanford, California: Stanford University Press, 1948. 159p. bibliog.

An excellent account of the laying of the telegraph line from Santiago to Valparaiso, which deals also with subsequent developments.

History. From independence to the War of the Pacific (1833-79)

146 **Commerce, credit and control in Chilean copper mining before 1880.**
John Mayo.   In: *Miners and mining in the Americas*. Edited by Thomas Greaves, William W. Culver. Manchester: Manchester University Press, 1985, p. 29-46.

A succinct survey, which is based, to a large extent, on primary sources, of the organization of the industry and the marketing of copper in the heyday of Chilean mining in the nineteenth century. The author highlights the industry's failure to create adequate technology to exploit lower grade ores when the more accessible seams ran out.

147 **The decline of a mining region and mining policy: Chilean copper in the nineteenth century.**
William W. Culver, Cornel J. Reinhart.   In: *Miners and mining in the Americas*. Edited by Thomas Greaves, William W. Culver. Manchester: Manchester University Press, 1985, p. 68-81.

This gives the reader a useful overview of the vicissitudes of the Chilean copper mining industry, which was the prop of the Chilean economy from the 1830s to the 1870s.

148 **Chile and the world depression of the 1870s.**
William F. Sater.   *Journal of Latin American Studies*, vol. 2, part 1 (May 1979) p. 67-99.

A vital article on Chilean economic history of the nineteenth century, based on primary research and including valuable statistical tables. The author emphasizes how far Chile's economic problems were part of a world-wide picture, the result of its integration into the international economy.

149 **William L. Oliver: un precursor de la fotografía. Chile en 1860.**
(William L. Oliver: a pioneer of photography. Chile in 1860.)
Alvaro Jara.   Santiago: Editorial Universitaria, 1973. 113p.

This quite splendid publication, by one of Chile's leading historians, is a reproduction of the remarkable photographs of William Oliver, an American photographer in Chile in 1860. Jara found the photographs in the Bancroft Library, and his text is an excellent accompaniment to this visual panorama of Chile in the period.

150 **Heirs of great adventure. The history of Balfour, Williamson and Company, Ltd.**
Wallis Hunt.   London: Balfour, Williamson, 1950-61. 2 vols.

Based on the company's rich archive and written by a former director, this is an amateur history of one of the most important British mercantile houses in Chile, from its foundation in 1850-51 to 1951. Despite the absence of footnotes, references and a bibliography, it is an interesting and competent narrative.

151 **Nitrates, Chilean entrepreneurs and the origins of the War of the Pacific.**
Luis Ortega. *Journal of Latin American Studies*, vol. 16, no. 2 (Nov. 1984), p. 337-80.

A scholarly account, based on archival material, including British commercial papers, considering the role of the Antofagasta Nitrate Company in the initiation of the War of the Pacific.

From the War of the Pacific to the modern age (1879-1964)

152 **Chile during the first few months of the War of the Pacific.**
William F. Sater. *Journal of Latin American Studies*, vol. 5, part 1 (May 1973), p. 133-58.

The myth that Chile won the War of the Pacific, against the combined forces of Peru and Bolivia, from a position of superior organization and national cohesion is partly exploded in this well-researched article. Chile, according to the author, was ill-prepared for war, with its economy in crisis and its leadership, both civil and military, indecisive. Fortunately for Chile, her adversaries were in an even worse position, so, in that sense, the myth is not entirely disproved.

153 **Chile and the War of the Pacific.**
William F. Sater.   Lincoln, Nebraska; London: University of Nebraska Press, 1986. 343p. bibliog.

Sater's is the best detailed account in English of a key episode in Chilean history. Basing his research on many primary sources, ranging from national archives to the national and provincial press, the author presents a convincing account which is also entertaining in its details of men and events. An impressive list of tables and a useful bibliography give added value to a fascinating narrative.

154 **Chili: sketches of Chili and the Chilians during the war, 1879-80.**
Robert Nelson Boyd.   London: W. H. Allen, 1881. 235p. map.

A contemporary account by a traveller which is particularly useful for its descriptions of economic activities, notably mining.

155 **Informes inéditos de diplomáticos extranjeros durante la Guerra del Pacífico.** (Unpublished reports of foreign diplomats during the War of the Pacific.)
Santiago: Editorial Andrés Bello, 1980. 437p.

Part of the centennial publications on the War of the Pacific (1879-83) between Chile on the one hand and Peru and Bolivia on the other, this collection of documents, culled from the foreign office archives of Germany, the United States, France and Great Britain, shows how their diplomatic representatives in Santiago saw the struggle. A very useful collection of documents which is primarily for the specialist.

156   **Boletín de la Guerra del Pacífico, 1879-1881.** (Bulletin of the War of the Pacific, 1879-81.)
      Santiago: Editorial Andrés Bello, 1979. 1205p. 14 maps.

A magnificently-produced facsimile reproduction of the official Chilean newsletter following the War of the Pacific as it progressed. It is indispensable as a printed documentary source for the study of the war, and was produced to mark the centenary of the outbreak of the war.

157   **Canciones y poesías de la Guerra del Pacífico, 1879.** (Songs and poetry of the War of the Pacific, 1879.)
      Juan Uribe Echevarría.   Santiago: Editorial Renacimiento, 1979. 321p.

Compiled to celebrate the centenary of the War of the Pacific, this is a superbly evocative collection of patriotic songs and poems of the period, with many reproductions of contemporary portraits, pictures and engravings, as well as drawings by Chile's outstanding modern cartoonist, Lukas.

158   **The nitrate industry and Chile's crucial transition: 1870-1891.**
      Thomas F. O'Brien.   New York, London: New York University Press, 1982. 211p. map. bibliog.

This valuable study of Chile's acquisition of the nitrate regions and of the significance of that development for her internal development is based on extensive archival research in both Chile and Great Britain. In particular, the author investigates the role of important business interests, both Chilean and British, in nitrates, and how that commodity became the pivot of the Chilean economy, and the highly significant political consequences of that development. It is an important book.

159   **Chile in the nitrate era: the evolution of economic dependence, 1880-1930.**
      Michael Monteón.   Madison, Wisconsin: University of Wisconsin Press, 1982. 256p. 2 maps. bibliog.

This book, which originated as a doctoral thesis, is a detailed examination of the interplay between Chilean politics and economics during the period when the nitrate industry dominated the country's economy. The author's main thesis is that Chile became a 'dependent' economy, given its subjection to foreign factors of production and sale of nitrate, and that this inhibited both its economic progress and its social development, establishing a pattern which would persist.

160   **Chilean elites and foreign investors: Chilean nitrate policy, 1880-1882.**
Thomas F. O'Brien, Jnr.   *Journal of Latin American Studies*, vol. 11, part 1 (May 1979), p. 101-21.

Based on archival research from private as well as public sources, this is an authoritative survey of the Chilean government's decision to return the nitrate industry to private hands after the War of the Pacific, which has been regarded by left-wing historians as a betrayal of the national interest. The author shows conclusively that that decision was not only the most pragmatic one in the circumstances but also coincided with the interests of the Chilean ruling class.

161   **British investments in the Chilean nitrate industry.**
J. Fred Rippy.   *Inter-American Economic Affairs*, vol. 8, no. 2, (autumn, 1954), p. 3-10.

This article examines, on the basis of printed sources including the contemporary press, the growth of the British stake in Chile's nitrate industry which it came to dominate. A pioneering piece, which has not been entirely superseded.

162   **The nitrate and iodine trades, 1880-1914.**
Robert Greenhill.   In: *Business imperialism, 1840-1930: an inquiry based on British experience in Latin America.* Edited by D. C. M. Platt. Oxford: Clarendon, 1977, p. 231-83.

A meticulously researched article, based largely on original material, which is concerned with the trade in nitrate and its by-product, iodine. In the period surveyed nitrate accounted for about half of the Chilean government's revenue. The author, a British economic historian with a special interest in Latin America, provides here a most valuable study.

163   **British nitrate companies and the emergence of Chile's proletariat, 1880-1914.**
Manuel A. Fernández.   In: *Proletarianisation in the third world. Studies in the creation of a labour force under dependent capitalism.* Edited by B. Munslow, H. Finch. London; Sydney; Dover, New Hampshire: Croom Helm, 1984, p. 42-76.

An excellent study of the social conditions of the nitrate workers in the period covered, which also looks at their response to their situation.

164   **The nitrate clippers.**
Basil Lubbock.   Glasgow: Brown, Son & Ferguson, 1932. 159p. map.

A detailed account, with numerous illustrations, of the clippers which carried nitrate from northern Chile to Europe for the German house of F. Laeisz and the French company of A. D. Bordes. Unfortunately, although it is clear that the work was researched carefully, there are no notes on sources, nor a bibliography.

History. From the War of the Pacific to the modern age (1879-1964)

165 **Agriculture and protectionism in Chile, 1880-1930.**
Thomas C. Wright. *Journal of Latin American Studies*, vol. 7, part 1, (May 1975), p. 45-58.

This is an excellent short study which challenges the traditional view that Chile's large landowners were free traders in the period between the War of the Pacific and the depression of the 1930s. The author proves, on ample records and useful tables, the view that they pressed for protectionist policies against foreign competition in pastoral and agricultural products.

166 **The annexation of Easter Island: geopolitics and environmental perception.**
J. Douglas Porteous. *North-South* (Canadian Journal of Latin American Studies), vol. 6, no. 11 (1981), p. 67-80. 3 maps.

It is not appreciated generally that Chile took part in the 'scramble' for Polynesia in the late nineteenth century, by annexing Easter Island, some 2,000 miles from Chile itself, in 1888. The author of this short but very interesting article is the leading contemporary authority on the island and here he discusses the reasons for the annexation.

167 **Dark days in Chile. An account of the revolution of 1891.**
Maurice H. Hervey. London: Edward Arnold; New York: Macmillan, 1892. 331p.

The special correspondent of *The Times* of London in Chile during the early months of the war provides an indispensable account of the revolution. Hervey was recalled because of his alleged partiality for President José Manuel Balmaceda. This is fascinating contemporary history.

168 **British nitrates and Chilean politics, 1886-1896: Balmaceda and North.**
Harold Blakemore. London: Athlone, 1974. 260p. map.

An extensively researched study, based on primary material, of the relationship between British predominance in Chilean nitrates, personified by John Thomas North, 'the nitrate king', and the politics of Chile under President José Manuel Balmaceda. It offers a basic interpretation of the origins, character and consequences of the Chilean revolution of 1891.

169 **Chilean revolutionary agents in Europe, 1891.**
Harold Blakemore. *Pacific Historical Review*, vol. 33, no. 4 (Nov. 1964), p. 425-46.

Using hitherto unpublished archival material on a little-researched aspect of the Chilean revolution of 1891, the author traces the activities of the agents of the Chilean congress, in revolt against President José Manuel Balmaceda, in Europe. Those activities ranged from a propaganda war and seeking diplomatic support to gun-running. The author suggests that the success of the agents was a major factor in the defeat of Balmaceda.

170 **Limitations of dependency: an historian's view and case study.**
Harold Blakemore. *Boletín de Estudios Latinoamericanos y del Caribe*, no. 18 (June 1975), p. 74-87.

This is an attack on some of the wilder protagonists of the 'dependency theory', using the affair of the Peruvian bondholders as an empirical case study, with research based largely on the British foreign office archives. The bondholders, consisting of foreign lenders to Peru in the 1870s, had their loans hypothecated on Peru's nitrate deposits in the Atacama desert. Peru had defaulted on its foreign loans early in the decade. When Chile seized the nitrate regions during the War of the Pacific (1879-83), the bondholders sought to hold Chile responsible for the repayment of Peru's debts. The article seeks to show how Chile successfully resisted powerful foreign pressure and asserted its independence on the issue.

171 **Emil Körner and the Prussianization of the Chilean army: origins, processes and consequences.**
Frederick M. Nunn. *Hispanic American Historical Review*, vol. 50, no. 2, (May 1970), p. 300-22.

In the 1880s, the Chilean government contracted with a Prussian senior officer, Körner, to raise the professional standards of the Chilean army. He did so and made it one of the best in Latin America. However, he quarrelled with his employer, President Balmaceda, and in the revolution of 1891, was the strategic brain behind Balmaceda's defeat. This is an excellent study of the man and his work by the leading authority on the Chilean military in English.

172 **Chilean politics, 1920-1931. The honorable mission of the armed forces.**
Frederick M. Nunn. Albuquerque, New Mexico: University of New Mexico Press, 1970. 219p.

The reputation of the Chilean armed forces – unlike that of most other services in Latin America's independent history – for non-intervention in political life was rudely shattered in 1924 when, against a background of political impasse, economic collapse and social disorder, they revolted aainst civilian rule and assumed power. Though civilian rule was restored in 1925, it was replaced in 1927 by the authoritarian government of General Carlos Ibáñez del Campo, a leading actor in 1924, establishing the nearest thing to a dictatorship in modern Chilean history before 1973. Ibáñez ruled until 1931 and the decade which saw his emergence is one of great historical controversy. Founded on extensive research, this book is without question the best account in English of that turbulent period, and is a detailed and essential study.

173 **Naval affairs in Chilean politics, 1910-1932.**
Philip Somervell. *Journal of Latin American Studies*, vol. 16, part 2, (Nov. 1984), p. 381-402.

The material for this article comes from both British and Chilean archives. It provides an interesting institutional study, tracing the roles and attitudes of the different sections of the Chilean navy in a time of great social and economic tension.

174 **Arturo Alessandri: a biography.**
Robert J. Alexander. Ann Arbor, Michigan: University
Microfilms International, 1977. 2 vols. bibliog.

A detailed, though, perhaps, over flattering political biography and survey of a
key figure of modern Chilean history, president of the Republic twice (1920-25
and 1932-38), by a well-known Latin Americanist in the United States. As well as
using his wide knowledge of sources, mostly secondary, the author has also drawn
upon personal interviews.

175 **The evolution of a socialist: Marmaduke Grove.**
Jack Ray Thomas. *Hispanic American Historical Review*, vol. 47,
no. 1, (Feb. 1967), p. 22-37.

Marmaduke Grove, one of Chile's first aviators, played a prominent part in the
military interventions of 1924 and 1925 and in the foundation of the Chilean
Socialist party in 1932. Though he was only very briefly in positions of high
authority, he played a prominent part in political events in the turbulent period of
the 1920s and 1930s. This short essay is a useful introduction to the man and his
times.

176 **Socialism and populism in Chile, 1932-52.**
Paul W. Drake. Urbana, Chicago; London: University of Illinois
Press. 1978. 418p. bibliog.

This is a quite outstanding piece of historical scholarship and undoubtedly the
best account in English of the fortunes of the Chilean Socialist party from its
foundation in 1932 to its temporary decline during and after the Second World
War. The author also adds a forty-page 'epilogue' on the party's history from 1952
to the military coup of 1973. As the bibliography indicates, it is heavily researched
and is, in many ways, as much a political history of Chile throughout the period as
a biography of the Socialist party *per se*. Essential reading on the period, the book
deservedly won a major prize for historical work in any one year in Latin
American history in the United States.

177 **Anti-parliamentary themes in Chilean history: 1920-70.**
H. E. Bicheno. *Government and Opposition*, vol. 7, no. 3
(summer 1972), p. 351–88.

A most important article, which traces the persistence of neo-Fascist ideologies,
movements and political groupings in Chilean politics. The author is concerned
only with the period from the first presidency of Arturo Alessandri to that of
Salvador Allende, but this work is of direct relevance to the contemporary
situation.

178 **Landowners and reform in Chile. The Sociedad Nacional de
Agricultura, 1919-1940.**
Thomas C. Wright. Urbana, Chicago; London: University of
Illinois Press, 1982. 249p. bibliog.

Founded in 1869 as a pressure group to defend the interests of large landowners
in Chile, the National Society of Agriculture was a major force in Chilean politics

for decades and still remains significant in the national life. This book, based upon research in relevant Chilean archives and an excellent knowledge of secondary works, is the best account in English of the activities of the society, especially of its responses to a growing tide of demand for agrarian reform in the period surveyed.

179 **External disequilibrium and internal industrialization: Chile, 1914-1935.**
Gabriel Palma. In: *Latin America: economic imperialism and the state*. Edited by Christopher Abel, Colin M. Lewis. London; Dover, New Hampshire: Athlone, 1985, p. 318-38. (University of London Institute of Latin American Studies Monographs, 13).

The author offers a challenging study of the Chilean economy during the period, rebutting traditional arguments on the 'positive' effects of the crisis of the early 1930s. He shows that there was a much higher degree of continuity through that period from what had gone before, and states that, in his view, the period was one of considerable development rather than regression.

180 **The Chilean Popular Front.**
John Reese Stevenson. Westport, Connecticut: Greenwood, 1942. 155p. bibliog.

Despite more recent research on Chilean politics in the 1930s, and on the formation of the Popular Front government, the first formal alliance of the left-wing and centre parties against the right, this near-contemporary account, based on many personal interviews as well as written sources, remains a valuable record of the period.

181 **The Seguro Obrero massacre.**
Richard R. Super. In: *The underside of Latin American history*. Edited by John F. Bratzel, Daniel M. Masterson. East Lansing, Michigan: Latin American Studies Center, Michigan State University, 1977, p. 43-66. (Monograph Series no. 16).

In 1938, the Chilean police massacred sixty-one young members of the national Nazi party, an event which shocked the country and contributed to the triumph of the Popular Front in that year's presidential election. It is assumed, but not categorically proved, that President Arturo Alessandri gave the fatal order. This is the most detailed account of the event in English.

Christian Democracy and Popular Unity (1964-73)

182 The last best hope: Eduardo Frei and Chilean democracy.
Leonard Gross.   New York: Random House, 1967. 204p.

A useful account of the rise of the Christian Democratic party in Chile and Frei's role in it, as the first president from that party. Written before Frei had completed his term, in 1970, it is now more useful as a prolegomenon to other, more substantial, works.

183 The rise and fall of Chilean Christian Democracy.
Michael Fleet.   Princeton, New Jersey: Princeton University Press, 1985. 274p. bibliog.

The rise of the Chilean Christian Democratic party from its real origins in the early 1930s to its place as the majority party in the system, with electoral victories in 1964 and 1965, is one of the phenomena of modern Chilean political history. Despite the fact that it has attracted a good deal of attention from historians and political scientists, particularly during the presidency of Eduardo Frei (1964-70), there are still not many convincing scholarly studies on the subject. The latest, however, makes a valuable contribution. It is particularly strong on the party's social basis and proves, indeed, how heterogeneous it was. It is also good on the government's achievements and on the divisions which emerged in the party hierarchy as the government experienced difficulties in the late 1960s. The argument that the author concludes with, however, which is reflected in his title, that the Pinochet period may strengthen the left and right, thus reducing the middle ground held by the party, may be premature.

184 Latin America: the hopeful option.
Eduardo Frei, translated by John Drury.   Maryknoll, New York: Orbis, 1978. 271p.

First published in Spanish in 1977, and here elegantly translated into English, this book reflects the basic thoughts of Latin America's first Christian Democratic president. It makes accessible to the English-speaking world what this distinguished Chilean statesman had expressed previously in his many writings in Spanish, and reveals him as not only a Christian but also a humanist, wise in world affairs.

185 Nationalism and Communism in Chile.
Ernst Halperin.   Cambridge, Massachusetts: Massachusetts Institute of Technology Press, 1965. 267p. bibliog. (Massachusetts Institute of Technology, Center for International Studies, Studies in International Communism, 5).

Written not long after the victory of the Christian Democratic party in the presidential election of 1964, this book is a useful piece of contemporary political analysis, focusing on the Chilean communist party but also analysing its relations

44

with its socialist ally and the challenge of its chief opponent, the Christian Democratic party. The strength of the book lies in its treatment of the impact of international events on domestic politics.

186 Chile's road to socialism.

Salvador Allende.   Harmondsworth, England; Baltimore, Maryland; Victoria, Australia: Penguin, 1973. 208p. (Pelican Latin American Library).

This translation of some of Allende's key speeches between 1969 and 1972 is a very useful documentary collection, illustrating not only his personal philosophy but also the aims of the government he led.

187 The Chilean road to socialism.

Edited by J. Ann Zammit.   London: Research Publications Services for the Institute of Development Studies of the University of Sussex, 1973. 465p.

This volume is a record of the proceedings of a nine-day conference, organized jointly by the Institute of Development Studies and ODEPLAN, the Chilean national planning office, held in Santiago in March, 1972. It was attended by economists and social scientists from all over the world, as well as by prominent Chileans from inside and outside government. As a presentation of the programme, progress and the expected prospects at that time of the socialist policies of Salvador Allende's Popular Unity government, it is a unique record.

188 Small earthquake in Chile. A visit to Allende's South America.

Alistair Horne.   London; Basingstoke: Macmillan, 1972. 335p. bibliog. map.

The account of a visit to Chile by a well-known British author at a time when the Popular Unity government, though embattled, seemed to be quite successful, this is a combination of travelogue and perceptive insight into the Chilean situation at that time. The author also visited other countries but his visit to Chile provides the core of the book. It is a fascinating account, embellished with numerous quotations from prominent Chileans he met and some excellent photographs.

189 Chile and Allende.

Edited by Lester A. Sobel.   New York: Facts on File, 1974. 190p.

A useful compilation which chronicles events in Chile from 1969 to early 1974. Based largely on newspaper reports and without interpretation, it provides a factual chronological account of the Allende régime and its overthrow.

190 Allende's Chile.

Edited by Philip O'Brien.   New York, Washington, London: Praeger, 1976. 296p. (Praeger Special Studies in International Politics and Government).

This is an interesting collection of essays covering politics, economics, agrarian reform, class structure, ideology and culture, the armed forces and relations with the United States. There is also a short epilogue on the subsequent military régime. The essays are written from a decidedly left-wing stance.

191 **The breakdown of democratic regimes: Chile.**
Arturo Valenzuela. Baltimore, Maryland; London: Johns Hopkins University Press, 1978. 140p. (The Breakdown of Democratic Régimes, vol. 4).

Undoubtedly one of the best accounts to date of the background to the military coup of 1973, written from the standpoint of a political scientist, and containing many useful statistical tables, the book is informed with a profound knowledge of Chilean society and politics.

192 **Chile, 1970-1973: economic development and its international setting. Self-criticism of the Unidad Popular government policies.**
Edited by S. Sideri. The Hague; Boston; London: Martinus Nijhoff, 400p.

The result of two seminars held at the Institute of Social Studies in the Hague in April and July, 1976, this is a very valuable collection of papers, giving a 'post-mortem' on the Popular Unity government of Salvador Allende. A prominent feature of the discussions was the participation of a number of ministers and other prominent supporters of the government. The inevitable rhetoric is counter-balanced by the frank acceptance of mistakes that were made.

193 **Coup! Allende's last day.**
José Manuel Vergara, Florencia Varas. New York: Stein & Day, 1975. 182p. 2 maps.

Written by a Chilean novelist and one of the country's best-known reporters, this is a gripping reconstruction of the events of the eleventh of September, 1973, the day when the armed forces overthrew the democratically-elected government of Salvador Allende. Based on eye-witness accounts, broadcasts and interviews, it is a valuable diary of a critical day in modern Chilean history.

194 **The overthrow of Allende and the politics of Chile, 1964-1976.**
Paul E. Sigmund. Pittsburgh: University of Pittsburgh Press, 1977. 326p. (Pitt Latin American Series).

Truly objective analyses of the overthrow of the Allende régime by the military in 1973 are not easy to find, given the impassioned circumstances of the event. This book, by a long-standing specialist on Chile with an intimate knowledge of the country, comes closer than many other works to a dispassionate study. The author sets the coup of 1973 into an historical context and provides a very reliable account of the Allende régime and its demise.

195 **Chile: the state and revolution.**
Ian Roxborough, Philip O'Brien, Jackie Roddick. London; Basingstoke: Macmillan, 1977. 304p. bibliog.

Written by three British social scientists, each of whom has considerable

46

experience of working in Chile, this is a valuable dissection of the Popular Unity government. It is written from a left-wing standpoint but is sufficiently objective to command respect, despite the additional drawback of a certain polemic tone, especially in the section on the subsequent military régime.

196 The last two years of Salvador Allende.
Nathaniel Davis. London: I. B. Tauris, 1985. 480p.

The author, as the ambassador of the United States to Chile during the last two years of the Allende régime, was in a distinctive positon to observe events, and this well-written and interesting narrative repays reading, not so much for what is new in it as for the recollections and attitudes of an observer who was sympathetic, in many ways, to Allende, while critical of many of the president's actions and methods. It reads as a frank narrative by an honest diplomat but one who, on his own evidence, may not have known what other agents of American policy were doing in Chile in his time.

197 Allende's Chile: an inside view.
Edward Boorstein. New York: International Publishers, 1977. 277p.

The author, an economist, was an adviser to Allende. His thesis is that the latter's government failed because it behaved hesitantly rather than in a revolutionary way, thus allowing the opposition time to develop. He is also critical of the faction-fighting within the government which dissipated its energies. A biased account from a left-wing viewpoint but one which is, nonetheless, worth reading.

198 Chilean voices: activists describe their experiences of the Popular Unity period.
Edited, recorded and translated by Colin Henfrey, Bernardo Sorj. Atlantic Highlands, New Jersey: Humanities Press, 1977. 197p. map.

Making use of translated and edited recordings of interviews with Chilean exiles after the military coup of 1973, the editors present a useful account of how some of the actors in the Allende period interpret the situation as it developed. It is strongly anti-American in tone, often to the point of polemic, but it has its uses, nevertheless.

199 Chile's Marxist experiment.
Robert Moss. Newton Abbot, England: David & Charles, 1973. 225p. bibliog.

Very few works in English on the Allende period, especially those written for the general public, are as distinctive as this one, which mounts a virtually unmitigated attack on the government of Popular Unity. Yet it is not a polemic work but the result of a serious investigation based on relevant material and on personal experience in Chile during the period. It provides a right-wing view but makes good narrative and, for those reasons, can be recommended as an interesting example of 'contemporary history', not least since it was published shortly after the military coup of 1973, when pro-Allende sentiment was at its height.

47

200 **Chile: the crime of resistance.**
Suzanne Labin. Richmond, England: Foreign Affairs Publishing,
1982. 282p.

First published in French in 1980, this is, together with the book by Robert Moss
(q.v.), one of the very few *apologias* for the military coup of 1973. It is an
unashamed indictment of the crimes and follies of the government of Salvador
Allende, passionately written but not entirely convincing. There is no bibliography and very few footnotes, though the writer has clearly read widely. It is
included here largely to counterbalance the plethora of books supporting the
opposite point of view.

201 **The tragedy of Chile.**
Robert Jackson Alexander. Westport, Connecticut: Greenwood,
1978. 509p. bibliog. (Contributions in Political Science, no. 8).

A well-known scholar of Latin American affairs, the author provides here a
compendious account of Chilean political and economic history from 1930 to
1977, concentrating on the years of Allende (1970-73) and the overthrow of his
régime. It is an objective and comprehensive analysis.

International Relations and Diplomatic History

202 **Analysing Chilean foreign relations.**
Manfred Wilhelmy. *Latin American Research Review*, vol. 17, no. 1 (1982), p. 244-54.

This review of three books and one article by a number of leading Chilean authorities on this subject has been written by a Chilean scholar who is himself an expert. It includes, therefore, discussion as well as description. The works themselves are wide-ranging, and the writer's summary of them, together with his critique, provides an admirable and concise survey of Chilean foreign affairs and also of the current state of the discipline in Chile.

203 **Social science in Chile: the Institute of International Studies of the University of Chile.**
Heraldo Muñoz. *Latin American Research Review*, vol. 15, no. 3 (1980), p. 186-89.

A useful descriptive note of the most important centre for the study of international affairs in Chile. Founded in 1966 and closely modelled on the British Royal Institute of International Affairs (Chatham House), the Institute has both a teaching and research programme, and publishes the important quarterly *Estudios Internacionales* (International Studies), one of the best Latin American-orientated journals in the field.

204 **Historia diplomática de Chile, 1541-1938.** (Diplomatic History of Chile, 1541-1938.)
Mario Barros van Buren. Barcelona: Ediciones Ariel, 1970. 781p. bibliog.

Written by a well-known Chilean diplomat, this large one-volume history of Chilean foreign affairs is essentially a chronological account, embellished with numerous illustrations, mostly portraits of important figures in Chilean diplomatic history. An important, if somewhat unexciting, survey of the subject.

205   **Cientocincuenta años de política exterior chilena.** (One hundred
      and fifty years of Chilean foreign policy.)
      Edited by Walter Sánchez, Teresa Pereira.   Santiago: Editorial
      Universitaria, 1979. 418p. bibliog. (Estudios Internacionales).

A valuable collection of essays, edited by two Chilean specialists on international
affairs, surveying the major issues in, and policies for, the conduct of Chilean
external affairs since independence.

206   **By reason or force: Chile and the balancing of power in South
      America, 1830-1905.**
      Robert N. Burr.   Berkeley; Los Angeles: University of California
      Press, 1965. 322p. map. bibliog. (University of California
      Publications in History, vol. 77).

This extensively researched book is a standard text on Chilean international
relations for the period it covers. The author demonstrates how successive
Chilean leaders were remarkably successful during the nineteenth century in
defining and defending national objectives and also highly accurate in evaluating
the policies of the other powers involved. It is, however, a pity that, in a book of
this kind, more maps were not included, given that so much of Chilean foreign
policy was concerned with boundary disputes with neighbouring countries.
Despite this, the book remains a basic work.

207   **Chile and the United States, 1880-1962: the emergence of Chile's
      social crisis and the challenge to United States diplomacy.**
      Fredrick B. Pike.   Notre Dame, Indiana: University of Notre
      Dame Press, 1963. 466p.

A remarkable attempt to interweave the domestic history of Chile with that of its
diplomatic relations with the United States, this book was written when the
Alliance for Progress had been launched but was still being tested. The author's
main thrust is that, for foreign policy towards Chile to be successful, American
policy-makers would need a more realistic assessment of Chile's social structure
and political evolution. This argument has not dated, and the book is a most
important contribution. The footnotes contain, in effect, an exhaustive survey of
Chilean historiography.

208   **Chile and its relations with the United States.**
      Henry Clay Evans, Jnr.   Durham, North Carolina: Duke
      University Press, 1927. Reprinted, New York: Johnson Reprint
      Corp, 1971. 243p. bibliog.

Though it only covers the period to 1930 and is, therefore, somewhat dated, this
is still a valuable survey of the diplomatic relations betwen Chile and the United
States, from the former's independence from Spain in the early years of the
nineteenth century.

209 **The last conquistadores: the Spanish intervention in Peru and Chile, 1863-1866.**

W. C. Davis.   Athens, Georgia: University of Georgia Press, 1950. 386p. bibliog.

A very detailed study of the war betwen Spain, on the one hand, and the Pacific coast republics on the other, which might be described as Spain's last attempt to assert her power in what had been her colonial empire.

210 **American diplomacy and the War of the Pacific.**

Herbert Millington.   New York: Columbia University Press, 1948. 172p. bibliog.

A detailed, if somewhat pedestrian, account, based on archival material, of the role of the United States in the war between Chile and the combined forces of Peru and Bolivia (1879-83), the results of which were to enlarge Chile's territory by about a third and to secure for it the nitrate wealth of the Atacama desert. The author carefully traces the history of fruitless American attempts to mediate in the conflict.

211 **The *Baltimore* affair.**

Joyce S. Goldberg.   Lincoln, Nebraska; London: University of Nebraska Press, 1987. 207p. bibliog.

Shortly after the Chilean revolution of 1891, sailors from the USS *Baltimore*, on shore-leave in Valparaiso, were involved in a fracas with a Chilean mob in which two sailors died, many were injured and a number imprisoned. The basic cause was anti-American sentiment, since the US Minister to Chile, Patrick Egan, was believed to have supported President Balmaceda against the victorious revolutionaries. The incident led to the most serious rift in US-Chilean relations which brought the two countries to the verge of war. This was averted but Chilean nationalism was aroused and anti-Americanism persisted. This is a clinical study of the affair, very well-documented with material from British, Chilean and American archives and contemporary newspapers.

212 **Chile y Gran Bretaña durante la primera guerra mundial y la postguerra, 1914–1921.** (Chile and Great Britain during the First World War and the post-war period, 1914-1921.)

Juan Ricardo Couyoumdjian.   Santiago: Editorial Andrés Bello, Ediciones Universidad Católica de Chile, 1986. 340p. bibliog.

The profound economic relationship between Chile and Great Britain from the time of the former's independence and the latter's decline in international economic importance has attracted much attention from historians. This detailed study of the crucial period in that relationship is a vital contribution to the understanding of the character and significance of that relationship, and is a remarkable work of scholarship, given the range of archival, press and secondary sources used. An important feature is the large number of statistical tables provided. The book is quite indispensable for the period and subject it covers.

213 **Tacna and Arica. An account of the Chile-Peru boundary dispute and of the arbitrations by the United States.**
William Jefferson Dennis. Hamden, Connecticut: Archon Books, 1967. 332p. 6 maps.

A reprint, in an unaltered and unabridged edition of the original version, published by Yale University Press in 1931, this is the classic account of the long-standing boundary dispute between Chile and Peru which began the War of the Pacific (1879-83) and was only resolved in 1929.

214 **Argentina and Chile: the struggle for Patagonia, 1843-1881.**
Richard O. Perry. *The Americas*, vol. 36, no. 3 (Jan. 1980), p. 347-63.

A useful historical survey of the disputes between Argentina and Chile over assumed rights in Patagonia and the Straits of Magellan. In both countries nationalists, and not least service personnel, have continued to argue the cases of each. Chile surrendered its claim to Patagonia in 1881, when, fighting Peru and Bolivia in the War of the Pacific, she needed Argentine neutrality to preserve her flank. However, scholars and others have argued that the claim should be renewed. The outstanding issue over islands in the Straits of Magellan was resolved by Papal mediation in 1984. This is a most helpful background article.

215 **A history of the Chilean boundaries.**
Robert D. Talbott. Ames, Iowa: Iowa State University Press, 1974. 134p. 4 maps. bibliog.

Much of Chile's diplomatic history has revolved around boundary disputes, with Argentina to the east and with Peru and Bolivia to the north. This is a useful history of those disputes down to 1974, with a good bibliography. It does not, of course, cover the final settlement of the Beagle Channel dispute with Argentina in 1984.

216 **The limits of hegemony: United States relations with Argentina and Chile during World War II.**
Michael J. Francis. Notre Dame, Indiana; London: University of Notre Dame Press, 1977. 292p. (Westview Special Studies in International Relations).

Based on archival research, largely in the State Department archives in Washington, DC, this diplomatic history of American relations with the two important South American states with sizeable pro-German minorities is an excellent study.

217 **Chilean Communists, radical presidents and Chilean relations with the United States, 1940-1947.**
Andrew Barnard. *Journal of Latin American Studies*, vol. 13, part 2, (Nov. 1981), p. 347-74.

Based on original material, including some from the archives of the Department of State, this article explores the relationship of Chilean governments under radical presidents with the United States during and after the Second World War. It also deals with the attitudes and actions of the Chilean Communist party as regards that relationship. A very useful article in both the diplomatic and the domestic history of modern Chile.

218 **The alliance for progress and Chile's 'revolution in liberty': 1964-70.**
Albert L. Michaels. *Journal of Inter-American Studies and World Affairs*, vol. 18, no. 1 (Feb. 1976), p. 74-99.

The Christian Democratic government of Eduardo Frei (1964-70) fitted perfectly into the Alliance for Progress, launched by President Kennedy in the early 1960s. That programme was intended to reduce the appeal of revolutionary doctrines in Latin America by providing economic assistance to democratic régimes. As the author cogently points out, however, it failed, not least because it was more successful in strengthening United States economic interests in Chile than in assisting fundamental reform. A well-argued contribution to the debate.

219 **The Harriman-Solomon mission and the 1966 Chilean copper agreement.**
David Berteau. In: *Economic coercion and US foreign policy, implications of case studies from the Johnson administration.* Edited by Sidney Weintraub. Boulder, Colorado: Westview, 1982, p. 173-214.

A detailed examination of the relations between Chile and the United States, during the Frei administration, over copper. The author demonstrates the pressure applied by the United States on Chile to ensure continued copper supplies at favourable prices during the Vietnam war.

220 **The rise and fall of project camelot: studies in the relationship between social science and practical politics.**
Edited by Irving Louis Horowitz. Cambridge, Massachusetts: MIT Press, 1974. 2nd ed. 409p.

The first edition appeared in 1967; this one, heavily revised, appeared after the military coup, when charges of United States involvement were widespread. Camelot was a project sponsored by the United States Department of Defence: it involved collaboration between social scientists from the United States and Chile for the analysis of social and other problems there. The revelation, in 1965, of the existence of that sponsorship resulted in an academic furore in both countries and also embittered their relations. This collection of essays is the definitive work on the episode.

221 **The United States and Chile: roots and branches.**
Richard R. Fagen. *Foreign Affairs*, vol. 53, no. 2 (1975), p. 297-313.

A critical but well-balanced appraisal of United States policy towards Chile, before and after the election of Salvador Allende in 1970, which attacks the open and the covert means used to discredit him.

222 **Latin American nations in world politics.**
Edited by Heraldo Muñoz, Joseph S. Tulchin.   Boulder,
Colorado: Westview, 1984. 278p. bibliog. (Foreign Relations of the
Third World, no. 3).

The result of a conference held in Santiago in 1982, this useful collection of essays
includes a study by Muñoz of the international policy of the Chilean Socialist
party from the Second World War to the fall of Allende (p. 150-67) and another
by Manfred Wilhelmy on politics, bureaucracy and foreign policy in Chile (p. 45-
62). These are very useful articles by two of Chile's leading authorities on the
country's international relations.

223 **Principled pragmatism in the face of external pressure: the foreign
policy of the Allende government.**
Carlos Fortín.   In: *Latin America: the search for a new
international role*. Edited by Ronald G. Hellman, H. Jon
Rosenbaum. Beverly Hills, California: Sage; New York: John
Wiley & Sons, Halstead Press Division, sponsored by the Center
for Inter-American Relations, 1975, p. 217-45. (Latin American
International Affairs Series, vol. 1).

An excellent summary of Chile's foreign policy during the Socialist government of
Salvador Allende by a prominent member of his régime who has been an exile
since the military coup of 1973. The author emphasizes, but dispassionately, the
impact of economic pressure from the United States. This was a constraint on the
freedom of action of the Allende government, and the author examines how it
sought to circumvent it.

224 **United States and Chile during the Allende years, 1970-73.**
United States Congress. House Committee on Foreign Affairs.
Sub-committee on Inter-American Affairs. 94th Congress, 1st
session, 1975.   Washington, DC: US Government Printing Office,
1975. 677p.

The report of hearings from 1971 to 1974, this is an indispensable source for
tracing the relations between the governments of the United States and Chile
during the turbulent presidency of Salvador Allende. American government
servants, businessmen and academics were interviewed, and the full, verbatim
testimony is provided. There is also a useful chronology.

225 **The United States and Chile: imperialism and the overthrow of the
Allende government.**
James F. Petras, Morris Morley.   New York: Monthly Review
Press, 1975. 217p. bibliog.

Although it was written fairly soon after the military coup of 1973 and has,
therefore, been overtaken in some respects by later works, this analysis, from a
Marxist viewpoint, nonetheless repays study. It deals with relations between the
two countries from the mid-1960s, focusing on American attempts to thwart
Allende's election in 1970 and also his programme. The authors underestimate

the role played by internal developments in Allende's fall but provide a strongly-argued attack on American policy.

226 **Allende's Chile and the Soviet Union: a policy lesson for Latin American nations seeking autonomy.**
Joseph L. Nogee, John W. Sloan. *Journal of Inter-American Studies and World Affairs*, vol. 21, no. 3 (Aug. 1979), p. 339-68.
A useful analysis of relations between Chile and the USSR during the Popular Unity government, emphasizing the economic aspects and concluding that, while Russia sympathized with Allende's programme, its practical assistance to an embattled economy was strictly limited and insufficient.

227 **Labyrinth.**
Taylor Branch, Eugene M. Popper. New York: Viking, 1982. 623p.
A highly detailed and intriguing account of the efforts of the government of the United States to get to the bottom of the assassination in Washington, DC, in September 1976, of Orlando Letelier, who was a leading opponent of the Pinochet régime. Very informative, not least on the issue of the involvement of persons at a high level and on the timidity of the United States government as regards pursuing those responsible.

228 **Persona non grata. An envoy in Castro's Cuba.**
Jorge Edwards. London; Sydney; Toronto: The Bodley Head, 1976. 275p.
Appointed by President Allende as Chile's first ambassador to Cuba after the resumption of diplomatic relations in 1970, the well-known Chilean writer and diplomat, Jorge Edwards, provides here a fascinating narrative of his experiences in Havana. During his short stay – he left in July, 1971 – he was at the centre of Chilean-Cuban relations, and despite the book's title he writes as much on Chile as on Cuba. A remarkable memoir by a remarkable man, the book is eloquently translated into English by Colin Harding.

229 **The Beagle Channel dispute: confrontation and negotiation in the southern cone.**
James L. Garrett. *Journal of Inter-American Studies and World Affairs*, vol. 27, no. 3 (fall, 1985), p. 81-109. bibliog. 2 maps.
An excellent survey of the history of the dispute, between Argentina and Chile, over three small islands in the Beagle Channel, a controversy which almost brought them to war in 1978 but was finally settled, through the mediation of the Pope, in 1984.

230 **Introduction to geopolitics.**
Augusto Pinochet Ugarte, translated from the Spanish by Liselotte
Schwarzenberg Matthei.   Santiago: Editorial Andrés Bello, 1983.
261p. bibliog.

Long before attaining his present position and, indeed, becoming head of Chile's
army before the coup in 1973, Pinochet's military career was made as a
geopolitician and lecturer at the Chilean military academy. This, the first English
translation of a work long in print in Spanish, reflects his preoccupation with
doctrines of national security against both external threat and internal subversion,
and consists largely of his notes and the analyses used in his teaching. It gives a
useful insight into his outlook and attitudes.

Ideas and Intellectual History

231 **Las ideas políticas en Chile.** (Political ideas in Chile.)
   Ricardo Donoso.   Buenos Aires: Eudeba, 1975. 3rd ed. 439p.
   bibliog.

First published in 1946, this book remains indispensable on the role of ideas in the evolution of Chile in the nineteenth century and demands an English translation.

232 **Andrés Bello. Philosopher, poet, philologist, educator, legislator, statesman.**
   Rafael Caldera, translated from the Spanish by John Street.
   London: George Allen & Unwin, 1977. 165p.

Though born a Venezuelan, Bello, one of the towering intellects of nineteenth-century Latin America, spent nearly half his life in Chile, mostly as a government servant. He founded the University of Santiago in 1842 and, until his death in 1865, produced a voluminous amount of writing, which is reflected in the title of this book. Its author, a former president of Venezuela, wrote it at the age of nineteen in the 1930s. Despite what has been written on Bello since, a *magnum opus* is still lacking. This can be highly recommended as an introduction to the life and work of a most remarkable man.

233 **Anthology of Andrés Bello.**
   Compiled by Pedro Grases, translated from the Spanish by
   Barbara D. Huntley, Pilar Liria.   Washington, DC: Department
   of Cultural Affairs, Organization of American States, 1981. 259p.

A very useful selection from the prodigious writings of Bello, the Venezuelan savant who made Chile his home. The selections include poetry as well as prose, the latter embracing his wide-ranging interests, including language, literary criticism, law, education, philosophy and journalism. The selections are annotated and there are notes on bibliographical sources and a listing of complete

57

editions of his works. The compilation was done by one of Venezuela's leading intellectuals, and has a foreword by Rafael Caldera.

234 **For God or country: history textbooks and the secularization of Chilean society, 1840-1890.**
Allen L. Woll. *Journal of Latin American Studies*, vol. 7, part 1 (May 1975), p. 23-43.

A fascinating essay on the debate in nineteenth-century Chile between liberals and conservatives, the anti- and pro-church parties, on what textbooks should be used in the educational system. The author shows how ideological positions took precedence over objective material.

235 **A functional past: the uses of history in nineteenth-century Chile.**
Allen L. Woll. Baton Rouge, Louisiana; London: Louisiana University Press, 1982. 211p.

No Latin American state has a finer historiographical tradition than Chile and, in relation to the country's size and population, so many distinguished historians. This is a solidly-based study of that characteristic of the national life which, as well as discussing the life and work of the leading figures, also shows how they influenced public policy and opinion.

236 **Positivism and history in nineteenth century Chile: José Victorino Lastarria and Valentín Letelier.**
Allen L. Woll. *Journal of the History of Ideas*, vol. 37, no. 3 (1976), p. 493-96.

A critical look at Chilean positivism, which is exemplified by two of Chile's leading intellectuals of the period. The author argues that because of intellectual divisions and the constraints imposed by the church, the Chilean positivists could not produce the 'scientific history' of Comte.

237 **Three Chilean thinkers.**
Solomon Lipp. Waterloo, Ontario: Wilfred Laurier University Press, 1975. 164p. bibliog.

The three thinkers, representing the intellectual outlook of their different generations, are Francisco Bilbao, the romantic democrat of the mid-nineteenth century. Valentín Letelier, a leading positivist of the end of the century, and Enrique Molina, representing the early twentieth-century reaction to the 'scientific' ideas of his intellectual fathers. This is a useful introduction to their philosophies, though more might have been said of the influence of Letelier and Molina in education as well as in thought.

238 **Barros Arana's *Historia jeneral de Chile*: politics, history and national identity.**
Gertrude Matyoka Yeager. Fort Worth, Texas: Texas Christian University Press, 1981. 187p. bibliog.

Diego Barros Arana (1830-1906) is generally regarded as the greatest historian produced by a country which is remarkable for the richness of its historiographical tradition. Much of his reputation rests on his massive sixteen-volume *General history of Chile* which appeared between 1884 and 1902. This book is not a biography but an attempt to argue, not very convincingly, that Barros Arana had conscious aims of an ideological nature in his work.

239 **Barros Arana, Vicuña Mackenna, Amunátegui: the historian as national educator.**
Gertrude Matyoka Yeager. *Journal of Inter-American Studies and World Affairs*, vol. 19, no. 2 (May 1977), p. 173-200.
An interesting essay on the impact of three leading Chilean historians of the last century and their role in the creation of political attitudes and civic values. All liberals, they had a considerable intellectual impact on younger generations of Chilean politicians and intellectuals. A well-researched and persuasive study.

240 **José Toribio Medina, his life and works.**
S. E. Roberts. Washington, DC: Inter-American Bibliographical and Library Association, 1941. 192p.
Medina (1852-1930) was not only one of Chile's most eminent historians, he was also the country's and, possibly, the world's, most outstanding bibliographer. His library, which he gave to the National Library in Santiago in 1925, is one of its chief adornments. This is a useful biography of one of Chile's most erudie scholars and one of the very few works on him in English. It has several appendixes; Appendix B lists works edited or translated by Medina, and Appendix C is a subject bibliography in nineteen sections.

241 **The reception of 'scientific sociology' in Chile.**
Edmundo F. Fuenzalida. *Latin American Research Review*, vol. 18, no. 2 (1983), p. 95-112.
Fuenzalida's is an interesting, though short, essay on the evolution of sociology as a social science in Chile, highlighting the significant contribution of individual scholars such as Eduardo Hamuy. It is based, to a large extent, on personal interviews.

242 **The heroic image in Chile: Arturo Prat, secular saint.**
William F. Sater. Berkeley, Los Angeles; London: University of California Press, 1973. 243p. bibliog.
Arturo Prat, captain of a Chilean ship during the War of the Pacific with Peru and Bolivia, is, perhaps, second only to Bernardo O'Higgins as a Chilean national hero, having lost his life dramatically in a battle with Peruvian ironclads. The author, on the basis of his extensive knowledge of both primary and secondary sources, provides a detailed account of how Prat's reputation was made. Of equal interest is his dissection of the opinions of succeeding Chilean generations about this enigmatic personality, which suggests that Prat became a symbol in national politics and, indeed, a reflection of them in a period of political crisis and social unrest. A fascinating study of the need of nations to believe in heroes, which shows how that need applies to Chilean experience.

243 **Nationalist movements and Fascist ideology in Chile.**
Jean Grugel. *Bulletin of Latin American Research*, vol. 4, no. 2
(1985), p. 109-22.

Short but interesting and a useful survey of currents of Fascist thought in Chilean
modern history, from the 1930s to the present day.

244 **Notes on authoritarian ideologies in Chile.**
Carlos Ruiz. *North-South* (Canadian Journal of Latin American
Studies), vol. 6, no. 11 (1981), p. 17-36.

An interesting analysis of the influence of Jaime Eyzaguirre, a leading Catholic
historian and thinker, whose writings, suggests the author, promoted authoritarian
ideas in tune with current ideologies. Eyzaguirre has had a profound impression
on many students at the Catholic University in Santiago. He died prematurely in a
car crash in 1967, but his ideas still carry weight.

Population

General

245 **Chilean social and demographic history: sources, issues and methods.**
Robert McCaa. *Latin American Research Review*, vol. 12, no. 2 (1978), p. 104-26.
An exemplary and provocative methodological article on Chilean population studies put into an historical context. This key article on the subject indicates the pitfalls for the social historian working on Chilean data and contributes not only fascinating material but also new ideas on methodology.

246 **Marriage and fertility in Chile: demographic turning points in the Petorca valley, 1840-1976.**
Robert McCaa. Boulder, Colorado: Westview, 1983. 207p. bibliog. maps. (Dellplain Latin American Studies, no. 14).
A highly sophisticated study, which uses computer methods, of marriage and fertility patterns in a carefully selected part of Chile, some 200 km. north of Santiago, from 1840 to 1976. A variety of primary records are used, as well as printed sources. It is outstanding, not only as a regional demographic investigation but also as a contribution to the methodology of the discipline.

Migration and migrants

247 **Bernardo Philippi, initiator of German colonization in Chile.**
George F. W. Young. *Hispanic American Historical Review*,
vol. 51, no. 3. (Aug. 1971), p. 478-96.

This is a useful biographical essay on the pioneer of German frontier settlement in
south-central Chile in the middle years of the nineteenth century. The wider
background of the movement is covered elsewhere. See also *Les Allemands au
Chili (1816-1945)* (q.v.) and *Germans in Chile: immigration and colonization,
1849-1919* (q.v.).

248 **Chile, Peru and the California gold rush of 1849.**
Jay Monaghan. London; Berkeley, Los Angeles: University of
California Press, 1973. 312p. bibliog.

Among the 'forty-niners' who rushed to California in the gold bonanza there were
considerable numbers of Chileans and Peruvians. At the same time, the Chilean
economy received a marked boost from the export of its wheat and flour to the
new Californian market. Based largely on press reports, this is an interesting and
sometimes 'racy' account of the episode, with twenty-two illustrations.

249 **Immigration and nationalism: Argentina and Chile, 1890-1914.**
Carl Solberg. Austin, Texas; London: University of Texas Press,
1970. 222p. 2 maps. bibliog. (Institute of Latin American Studies,
Monograph no. 18).

This comparative study looks at the impact of foreign immigration and national
reactions to it in the two countries, at an important time for their economic
development. Though based on printed material, rather than primary sources, it
is an important contribution, the Chilean material being of considerable interest
to the historian of migration in general.

250 **Recent colonization in Chile.**
Mark Jefferson. New York: American Geographical Society,
1924. 52p. (Research Series no. 6).

Despite the date of publication, this remains a valuable study of immigration into
Chile and especially the settlement of south-central provinces.

251 **Urban migration and economic development in Chile.**
Bruce H. Herrick. Cambridge, Massachusetts; London:
Massachusetts Institute of Technology Press, 1965. 126p.
(Massachusetts Institute of Technology Economics Monograph
Series no. 6).

Though now, of course, somewhat dated, this study of internal Chilean migration
in the 1950s and 1960s still has value for the geographer and social scientist. It
concentrates on inward migration to the capital, Santiago – which contains about
a third of the national population – indicating that rural migration was a minor

factor in its growth in this period, most of the migrants coming from cities. Some thirty statistical tables enhance its value.

252   **A study on immigrations to greater Santiago (Chile).**
Juan C. Elizaga.   *Demography*, vol. 3, no. 2 (1966), p. 353-77.

Based on a survey undertaken by the Latin American Demographic Centre (CELADE) in 1962, this is an important article on migration to the capital from other parts of Chile. The data came from a sample of 2,000 households in Greater Santiago, which contains a third of all Chileans, and the study, replete with tables, is concerned with a history of internal migration; the motives of migrants; their movements within the city over time; age, sex and housing patterns; and comparisons with those born in the capital. Although, naturally, dated, it is still useful for the understanding of internal migration in Chile.

Minorities

253   **Les Allemands au Chili (1816-1945).** (The Germans in Chile, 1816-1945.)
Jean-Pierre Blancpain.   Cologne: Böhlau Verlag, 1974. 1162p. bibliog.

A very significant minority in the Chilean population, whose contribution to national development has been out of all proportion to its numbers, the German-born population has been the subject of a number of academic studies. It is unlikely, however, that this book will ever be superseded. Its sources, exemplified by an extraordinarily detailed bibliography, are comprehensive and the detail of the narrative a classic illustration of the French *Annales* school. An exemplary work of historical scholarship, which contains a useful appendix of photographs.

254   **Germans in Chile: immigration and colonization, 1849-1919.**
George F. W. Young.   New York: Center for Migration Studies, 1974. 234p. bibliog. 7 maps.

Though considerably less detailed than the extraordinary book by J. P. Blancpain (q.v.) on the subject of German immigration into Chile and the colonization of what was then the southern frontier, this is the best work in English on the part played by that significant minority in the making of modern Chile. There is an excellent bibliography.

255   **German colonies in South America: a new Germany in the Cono Sur?**
Hans Werner Tobler, Peter Waldemann.   *Journal of Inter-American Studies and World Affairs*, vol. 22, no. 2 (May 1980), p. 227-45.

In effect a review article, this looks at four books on German immigration in

Population. Minorities

Chile, Argentina and Brazil, all countries where German immigrants have played a role in society, economy and politics which is quite incommensurate with their size. A valuable article which assesses the impact of the immigrants, their adaptation to the host countries, and their influence on them.

256 **The political emergence of Arab-Chileans, 1952-58.**
Donald W. Bray. *Journal of Inter-American Studies*, no. 4 (Oct. 1962), p. 557-62.
This article is a useful addition to the sparse literature, in English, on ethnic minorities in Chile. Throughout Latin America, Middle Eastern immigrants have made a contribution, in both business and politics, which is out of proportion to their numbers. Chile is no exception, and, though brief, this is an interesting article.

257 **Jews of the Latin American republics.**
Judith Larkin Elkin. Chapel Hill, North Carolina: University of North Carolina Press, 1980. 298p. bibliog.
A very interesting study of the Latin American aspect of the greatest diaspora in world history. Although the number of Jews in Chile has been less than in Brazil and Argentina, those present have contributed, though not without nationalistic criticism, to Chile's economic development. The major influx occurred in the 1930s, a consequence of the rise of Fascist ideologies in Europe.

258 **Historia de la comunidad israelita sefaradí de Chile.** (History of the Jewish sephardic community in Chile.)
Moshé Arueste. Santiago: Editorial Nascimento, 1984. 385p. bibliog.
This is an exhaustive account of the small but influential Jewish community in Chile. As elsewhere, its members have been prominent in cultural and busines activities to a degree quite incommensurate with their numbers. The author subsequently emigrated to Israel, changing his name to Moshé Nes-El.

259 **Yugoslav immigrant experiences in Argentina and Chile.**
Victor C. Dahl. *Inter-American Economic Affairs*, vol. 28, no. 3 (winter 1974), p. 3-26.
A very useful and well-documented account of approximately 25,000 Yugoslavs, who settled in Chile in the late nineteenth and early twentieth centuries, mostly in the southernmost parts of the country.

260 **The Anglo-Chilean community.**
L. C. Derrick-Jehu. *Family History*, vol. 3, nos. 17-18 (Nov. 1965), p. 157-84.
The British influence in the evolution of Chile after independence was enormous, and a major part was played by British immigrants, mostly in business, who married Chileans. Their descendants have been prominent in government and politics, business and society and include such names as Edwards, Blest, MacIver,

Ross and Williams. This article, which is really a collection of biographies, is valuable because there is little on the subject in English, despite its importance and fascination.

Women

261 **Sex and class in Latin America.**
Edited by June Nash, Helen Safa.   New York; London: Praeger, 1976. 330p. bibliog.

This volume of interesting essays contains three that are devoted specifically to Chile, by Jorge Gissi Bustos, Michèle Mattelart and Ximena Bunster. The discussion is primarily of political and cultural aspects, and includes an unusual study of a successful Mapuche woman.

262 **Supermadre. Women in politics in Latin America.**
Elsa M. Chaney.   Austin, Texas: University of Texas Press, 1979. 210p. bibliog. (Institute of Latin American Studies, Latin American Monographs, no. 50).

An excellent study of women in politics in Peru and Chile, which shows how women in positions of influence have achieved these by specializing in tasks that epitomize the mother's role, such as health and education.

263 **Women in Latin American politics: the case of Chile and Peru.**
Elsa M. Chaney.   In: *Female and male in Latin America: essays.* Edited by Ann Pescatello. Pittsburgh, Pennsylvania: University of Pittsburgh Press, 1973, p. 103-39.

On the basis of field-work of the late 1960s, this article, by an authority on women in Latin America, looks at the factors which have determined women's participation in politics in the two countries considered. It is a largely descriptive article, but useful in its coverage of female voting patterns and party affiliations. The author's book (q.v.) includes this material and also the material in *Old and new feminists in Latin America: the case of Peru and Chile* (q.v.), but readers wishing to focus on female political behaviour in Chile will find both articles the best introduction.

264 **Old and new feminists in Latin America: the case of Peru and Chile.**
Elsa M. Chaney.   *Journal of Marriage and the Family*, vol. 35, no. 2 (May 1973), p. 331-43.

Here, Chaney compares the historical evolution of feminist movements, in the two countries surveyed, since the latter part of the nineteenth century. The overall conclusion is that, while advances have been made in women's rights in both, national culture is still dominated by males, a situation which seems likely to continue.

265 **Chile: mujer y sociedad.** (Chile: woman and society.)
Compiled by Paz Covarrubias, Rolando Franco.
Santiago: United Nations Children's Fund, 1978. 876p. bibliog.

This is the most comprehensive collection of essays on women in Chilean society, consisting of thirty-two contributions by forty authors, covering every aspect of the subject, such as women in the labour force, family planning, religious attitudes, the feminist movement, the media's images of women and the legal status of women.

266 **La mujer en el reino de Chile.** (Women in the kingdom of Chile.)
Imelda Cano Roldán. Santiago: Municipalidad de Santiago, 1981.
680p. bibliog.

An exhaustive account of women in colonial Chile, covering their roles, activities, education, occupations, and so on. It offers a wealth of information, based, essentially, on hitherto unpublished sources.

267 **Forgotten females: women of African and Indian descent in colonial Chile, 1536-1800.**
Della M. Flusche, Eugene H. Korth. Detroit, Michigan: Blaine Ethridge, 1983. 112p.

Aimed at the non-specialist reader and using printed sources, this is an interesting study of non-Spanish women in Chile during the colonial period. One chapter deals with the Indian princess of Inca origin, Beatriz Clara Coya, who married the Spanish governor, Oñez de Loyola.

268 **Tres ensayos sobre la mujer en Chile: siglos XVIII-XIX-XX.** (Three essays on women in Chile: eighteenth, nineteenth and twentieth centuries.)
Lucía Santa Cruz, Teresa Pereira, Isabel Zegers, Valera Maino.
Santiago: Editorial Universitaria, 1978. 328p.

Despite being a richly illustrated book and a useful addition to a subject on which very little has been written, this is an uneven work. The chapters on the period before the twentieth century lack depth, relying too much on the, mostly male, chroniclers' and travellers' opinions. However, given the paucity of books on this neglected topic, and considering that women have played a very significant and so far unacknowledged role in Chilean history, it is a welcome, and well-produced, addition to the literature.

269 **Women's roles in nineteenth-century Chile: public education records, 1843-1883.**
Gertrude Matyoka Yeager. *Latin American Research Review*, vol. 18, no. 3 (1983), p. 149-56.

A short but useful article on a much-neglected topic, emphasizing the significance of sources on the education of women during the last century as a basic tool for research into women's studies.

270 **La mujer chilena (el aporte feminino al progreso de Chile) 1910-1960.** (The Chilean woman (the female contribution to the progress of Chile) 1910-1960.)
Felícitas Klimpel. Santiago: Editorial Andrés Bello, 1962. 304p.
An interesting survey of the role of women in Chilean public life and culture in this period. The legal position of Chilean women is discussed and there are extensive lists of names of women in the professions and the arts. Given the shortage of such studies, this is a very useful book.

271 **Women in Chile: yesterday and today.**
Catalina Palma. London: Chile Solidarity Campaign, 1984. 21p.
A short but useful survey of the historical background of the struggle for women's rights in Chile which emphasizes male dominance of the political system.

272 **Voting in Chile: the feminine response.**
Steven M. Neuse. In: *Political participation in Latin America*. Edited by John A. Booth, Mitchell A. Seligson. New York: Holmes & Meier, 1979, p. 129-44.
This is an interesting analysis of women's voting patterns, 1932-73, showing how women became increasingly independent of male influence, and how political parties sought to mobilize their higher degree of participation.

273 **Yo trabajo así . . . en casa particular.** (That is how I worked . . . in a private house.)
Thelma Gálvez, Rosalba Todaro. Santiago: Centro de Estudios de la Mujer (CEM), 1985. 113p.
About one quarter of Chilean women who are in employment work as domestic servants. This book is, in effect, a transcript of interviews with four such women. It paints a vivid picture of their lives, expectations and frustrations, through their daily occupation. Although the transcripts are left without comment or judgement, they provide a moving testimony of the female domestic servant in Chile.

274 **Scraps of life. Chilean women under Pinochet.**
Marjorie Agosín, translated from the Spanish by Cola Franzen. London: Zed Books, 1987. 160p. (Latin America / Women's Studies series).
The writer, a Chilean poetess who now teaches in the United States, has written an eloquent and moving account of the Chilean working-class women of Santiago who, after the military coup of 1973, made their living by making collages of pieces of coloured cloth sewn on to sacking, known as *arpilleras*. The book is both an account and a tribute.

275   **Female migration in Chile: types of moves and socioeconomic characteristics.**
Joan M. Herold.   *Demography*, vol. 16, no. 2 (May 1979), p. 257-78. bibliog.

Based on a five per cent sample of the Chilean census of 1970, this interesting article examines internal female migration in the period 1965-70. It is a closely researched piece, describing the characteristics of migrant women in terms of age, education, work and directions of movement, which suggests that, perhaps paradoxically, female urban migration is more a characteristic of upper than lower-class women.

Religion

276 **The Church and politics in Chile: challenges to modern Catholicism.**
Brian H. Smith.   Princeton, New Jersey: Princeton University
Press, 1982. 383p. bibliog.

This book is, without doubt, the most important study in English of the Catholic
Church in Chile and its relationship to Vatican policy, to Chilean social issues and
to the major political parties. Based on a very impressive list of sources, including
oral interviews and the author's own experience as a priest in Santiago, it
concentrates on the period from the 1920s to the early 1980s, and is quite
indispensable for the understanding of the Church in Chile and also of the
dilemmas posed to the church in the face of social distress and authoritarian
government.

277 **A yankee reformer in Chile: the life and works of David Trumbull.**
Irven Paul.   South Pasadena, California: William Carey Library,
1973. 155p. bibliog.

Trumbull (1845-89) was a Protestant missionary in Chile and an outstanding figure
in its non-Catholic religious history. This is a good biography of a remarkable
man which also has much relevant material on the relations between Church and
State, a key issue in nineteenth-century Chilean history.

278 **Followers of the new faith: cultural change and the rise of
Protestantism in Brazil and Chile.**
Emilio Willems.   Nashville, Tennessee: Vanderbilt University
Press, 1967. 290p.

A valuable comparative study which deals with the rise of the Protestant faith in
what are basically Catholic countries. Although more than two-thirds of all
Chileans profess the Roman Catholic faith, historically, Church-State relations
have often been turbulent. This was so, particularly, in the nineteenth century,

69

Religion

when Protestant churches were established by permission, partly reflecting the presence in Chile of small, but significant, non-Catholic immigrant minorities. The author is concerned, mainly, with how modern processes of change, such as industrialization, urbanization and secularization, have affected the balance of faiths in Chile.

279 **Los cristianos por el socialismo en Chile.** (The Christians for socialism in Chile.)
Teresa Donoso Loero.   Santiago: Editorial Vaitea, 1976. 3rd ed. bibliog.
This well documented and illustrated book gives a detailed account of one of the most interesting movements in the religious life of modern Chile, namely that of the Christians who supported the Marxist government of Salvador Allende. A most useful section consists of brief biographies of the principal actors in the story.

280 **Women religious, the poor and the institutional church in Chile.**
Katherine Anne Gilfeather. *Journal of Inter-American Studies and World Affairs*, vol. 21, no. 1 (Feb. 1979), p. 129-55. bibliog.
An interesting study of the 'theology of liberation' in Chile, particularly as it has affected women, both religious and lay, written by a Maryknoll nun, who is fairly critical of the Chilean hierarchy for its conservative attitudes, though these have changed somewhat since the article was written. It is still valuable since the issues addressed are of current and future concern.

281 **The Church and the process of democratization in Latin America.**
Hugo Villelo G. *Social Compass*, vol. 26, nos. 2-3 (1979), p. 261-84.
Despite its general title, the research which forms the basis of both specific material and general hypotheses was conducted in Chile. This is an important article on the ways in which the Church has recently evolved, in both its political and social outlook.

282 **Alliance or compliance: implications of the Chilean experience for the Catholic Church in Latin America.**
Virginia Marie Bouvier. Syracuse, New York: Syracuse University, Maxwell School of Citizenship & Public Affairs, 1983. 105p. bibliog. (Latin American Series no. 3).
Set against the broad background of the changing attitudes of the Catholic Church in Latin America, which is moving towards a more reformist stance, this is a useful study of the relationship between Church and State in Chile, with emphasis on the period since the military coup of 1973.

283   **The Catholic Church under a military régime.**
Thomas G. Sanders, Brian H. Smith.   In: *Military government
and the movement towards democracy in South America.* Edited by
Howard Handelman, Thomas G. Sanders. Bloomington,
Indiana: Indiana University Press, 1981, p. 307-45.
Following the suspension of political activity after the military coup of 1973, it fell
largely to the Church to act as the national conscience against abuses of human
rights and the effects of economic policies on the poor. Written by two
acknowledged authorities in the field of Church-State relations in Latin America,
this is an excellent summary of the situation.

284   **Chile: la Vicaría de la Solidaridad.** (Chile: the Vicariate of
Solidarity.)
Juan I. Gutiérrez Fuente.   Madrid: Alianza, 1986. 232p.
The suppression of political activity after the military coup of 1973, followed by
the widespread abuses of human rights, and the economic plight of those affected
most by the government's economic policies evoked the concern of the Roman
Catholic Church in Chile. The Church, however, had to tread warily in its
dealings with government and the *Vicaría de la Solidaridad* emerged. This has
remained the most active organization, with a wide variety of activities, ranging
from protection and surveillance in human rights issues to provision of food to
the poor. This account of its activities, and the remarkable people who run it,
deserves a wider audience than the Spanish-speaking world alone.

Society and Social Conditions

General

285 **Research methods for the analysis of the internal structure of dominant classes: the case of landlords and capitalists in Chile.**
Maurice Zeitlin, Richard Earl Ratcliff. *Latin American Research Review*, vol. 10, no. 3 (1975), p. 5-61.

Essentially Marxist, this analysis of Chilean upper-class society and its economic interests, suggests new methodological tools to aid the understanding of the subject. Several valuable tables on family interrelationships reinforce the text. This is a provocative piece of research for the social historian, which emphasizes the significance of kinship is a major key to the understanding of Chilean society.

286 **Family clusters: generational nucleation in nineteenth-century Argentina and Chile.**
Diana Balmori, Robert Oppenheimer. *Comparative Studies in Society and History*, vol. 22, no. 2 (April 1979), p. 231-61.

Based on research in notarial and judicial archives, as well as biographical dictionaries, this is a valuable contribution to the study of family relationships and regional control. In both countries, particularly Chile, kinship is a fundamental key for understanding the history and politics.

287 **Social policies in Chile: an historical review.**
José Pablo Arellano. *Journal of Latin American Studies*, vol. 17, no. 2 (Nov. 1985), p. 397-418.

This gives a valuable historical overview of the social policies of successive Chilean governments over the last eighty years.

288 **Social security in Latin America. Pressure groups, stratification and inequality.**
Carmelo Mesa-Lago.   Pittsburgh, Pennsylvania: University of Pittsburgh Press, 1978. 351p. (Pitt Latin American Series).

Very little has been written in a scholarly form in English on this subject, and the section on Chile (p. 22-69) is a most valuable survey, though, inevitably, dated by the military coup of 1973 which, among other things, led to drastic changes in the social security system. The author succinctly traces the historical evolution of that system to the early 1970s and provides much useful statistical data.

289 **Change and frustration in Chile.**
Osvaldo Sunkel.   In: *Obstacles to change in Latin America*.
Edited by Claudio Véliz.   London, New York: Oxford University Press, 1965, p. 116-44.

A first-rate 'overview' of Chilean economic, social and political problems as the Christian Democratic government of Eduardo Frei took office. A reflective essay, which is not as dated as it might seem.

290 **The state and formation of a middle class: a Chilean example.**
Geraldine Grant.   *Latin American Perspectives*, vol. 10, nos. 2-3 (spring and summer 1983), p. 151-70.

The first half of this article deals broadly with the growth of the middle class between 1930 and 1973 and the second with the case study of the southern province of Cautín. The article is not without errors, but there are so few such regional studies in English that this one repays reading.

291 **Class conflict and economic development in Chile: 1958-1973.**
Barbara Stallings.   Stanford, California: Stanford University Press, 1978. 295p.

This study compares the three presidencies which Chile experienced between 1958 and 1973 – the 'business' government of Jorge Alessandri, the 'moderate' reforming régime of Eduardo Frei and the socialist administration of Salvador Allende. The approach is Marxist in terms of its complex class analysis, but the book merits serious reflection, no matter what the reader's ideological standpoint.

292 **Manuel.**
Christopher Jackson.   London: Cape, 1965. 223p.

A graphic, indeed horrifying, account of a boy prostitute in Chile who attained notoriety in 1962 when he murdered a middle-aged lawyer in Valparaiso. Based both on Manuel's own interviews with the author and on the testimony of his fellow-prisoners, the book is a stark indictment of the Chilean penal system at that time and also of the social conditions which made Manuel a victim of it.

293 **Vulnerable groups in recessionary situations: the case of children and the young in Chile.**
Alejandro Foxley, Dagmar Raczynski. *World Development*, vol. 12, no. 3 (March 1984), p. 223-46. bibliog.
A well-known Chilean economist and an equally esteemed sociologist discuss the effects of the deep economic recession on the young in the early 1980s. They evaluate the various emergency measures adopted to shield the younger age groups, emphasizing that, while infant mortality actually fell in the period, the overall situation of the young declined.

Housing and urbanization

294 **Historia urbana del reino de Chile.** (The urban history of the kingdom of Chile.)
Gabriel Guarda. Santiago: Editorial Andrés Bello, 1978. 509p. bibliog.
This is a truly extraordinary compilation by one of Chile's leading historians of the colonial period. It gives the fullest account to date of the cities and towns established in Chile between 1540 and 1826, and is unlikely to be superseded. It is illustrated lavishly with over 400 drawings, reproductions of maps in archives and photographs. The bibliography, of over 4,600 items, is also remarkable in itself. A quite outstanding work.

295 **Desarrollo urbano de Santiago (1541-1941.)** (The urban development of Santiago, 1541-1941.)
René Martínez Lemoine. *Revista Paraguaya de Sociología*, vol. 15, nos. 43-44 (May-Dec. 1978), p. 57-90.
A survey of the growth of Chile's capital, from its foundation by Pedro de Valdivia to its 400th anniversary.

296 **Military influence in the cities of the kingdom of Chile.**
Gabriel Guarda. In: *Urbanization in the Americas from its beginnings to the present.* Edited by Richard P. Schaedel, Jorge E. Hardoy, Nora Scott Kinzer. The Hague: Mouton, 1978, p. 343-82.
An essay on urbanization in colonial Chile by a leading authority, the article concentrates on the forts of southern Chile on the Indian frontier as incipient cities beginning as garrison towns. Information is provided on a number of these cities, such as Valdivia and Nacimiento.

297 **Chilean housing experience.**
Edwin Harmoto. *Planning Outlook*, vol. 21, no. 1 (1978),
p. 16-77. bibliog.

This article gives a useful survey of the factors conditioning housing in Chile from
the late 1950s to the date of publication.

298 **Squatters and politics in Latin America: a comparative analysis of
urban social movements in Chile, Peru and Mexico.**
M. Castells.   In: *Towards a political economy of urbanization in
Third World countries*. Edited by H. I. Safa. Oxford: Oxford
University Press, 1982, p. 249-82.

A leading Marxist student of urbanization, a process in which Latin America,
including Chile, leads the world, offers here a valuable inter-country comparison
of the relationship, in these three countries, between slum settlements and the
politicization of their inhabitants.

299 **Campamento.** (Camp.)
Monica Pidgeon.   *Architectural Design*, no. 12 (1972), p. 739-45.
map.

The *campamentos* are Chile's shanty towns, which are also known by other
names. This well-illustrated article is concerned with the attempts of the Allende
government to reduce them by setting a target of 80,000 new housing units to be
completed by the expected end of Allende's period of office. This would have left
a considerable number of people still living in the *campamentos*, since in 1970 it
was estimated that they held over 90,000 people, for whom seventy per cent of
the new units were to be set aside. In the late 1980s, it is estimated that the
number of shanty-town dwellers has risen dramatically, although precise statistics
are not available.

300 **A decade of struggle for housing in Chile.**
Richard T. LeGates.   *Inter-American Economic Affairs*, vol. 28,
no. 2, (autumn 1974) p. 51-75.

A succinct survey of the housing programmes of the governments of Eduardo Frei
(1964-70) and Salvador Allende (1970-73), which is all the more useful when one
considers the paucity of works in English on the subject of housing in Chile.

301 **Urban regional policies for national development in Chile.**
John Friedmann.   In: *Latin American urban research, vol. 1*.
Edited by Francine F. Rabinovitz, Felicity M. Trueblood.
Beverly Hills, California: Sage Publications, 1971, p. 217-45.

Though obviously not up-to-date, this is nonetheless a valuable survey by a well-
known authority, of the urbanization of Chile and its problems during the 1960s.
The writer considers planning policies at that time and how successfully they were
carried out, as well as making recommendations for the future. His emphasis on
regional development, however, has been contradicted, in part, by the military
régime, in power since 1973, which has underlined the strong centralism which
has always characterized the country's evolution, despite its shape.

Society and Social Conditions. Housing and urbanization

302 **Housing policies or housing politics: an evaluation of the Chilean experience.**
Fernando Kuznetsoff. *Journal of Inter-American Studies and World Affairs*, vol. 17 (1975), p. 281-301.
An interesting comparison of the housing policies of two contrasting Chilean régimes, the Christian Democratic and Popular Unity, showing the relationship between those policies and national politics.

303 **Housing the urban poor in Chile: contrasting experiences under 'Christian Democracy' and 'Unidad Popular'.**
Eduardo P. Lozano. In: *Latin American urban research*, Vol. 5, *Urbanization and inequality: the political economy of urban and rural development in Latin America.* Edited by Wayne A. Cornelius, Felicity M. Trueblood. Beverly Hills, California; London: Sage Publications, 1975, p. 177-94.
A study contrasting the policies of popular housing under the two governments, indicating that the Popular Unity government had a closer interest in the political benefits to be gained from ambitious programmes than its predecessor, but showing that, although it had high targets, its programmes were not technically feasible.

304 **Urban and housing policies under Chile's military dictatorship, 1979-1985.**
Fernando Kuznetzoff. *Latin American Perspectives*, vol. 14, no. 33. (spring 1987), p. 157-86.
In many respects this can be used as a continuation of the preceding item, bringing the subject up-to-date by considering the Pinochet régime's record on housing in its first ten years.

305 **The lessons and legacy of a dark decade.**
Steven Volle. New York: North American Congress on Latin America, *NACLA report on the Americas*, vol. 17, no. 5 (Sept.-Oct. 1983), p. 7-14.
A critical review of Chilean housing policies and achievements, under the military régime, since 1973, illustrated with photographs.

306 **Chilean regional development policy.**
Manuel Achurra Larraín. In: *Latin American urban research*, vol. 2. *Regional and urban development policies: a Latin American perspective.* Series editors: Francine M. Rabinovitz, Felicity M. Trueblood; vol. editors: Guillermo Geisse, Jorge E. Hardoy. Beverly Hills, California; London: Sage Publications, 1972, p. 133-41.
A short but useful summary of Chilean experiences of regional development, focusing on the late 1960s and emphasizing the role of the state planning agency

76

(ODEPLAN) and the establishment of new machinery for regional development, based, in part, on urban growth poles.

307 **Services in the contemporary Latin American city: the case of Chile.**
Markos Mamalakis. In: *Urbanization in the Americas from its beginnings to the present.* Edited by Richard P. Schaedel, Jorge E. Hardoy, Nora Scott Kinzer. The Hague: Mouton, 1978, p. 303-12.

This is an economist's survey of such factors as banking, investment in services and income distribution in the urbanization process in Chile. It is, however, rather too technical for the layman. The article stresses, correctly, that the concentration of services in urban areas and the use of the governmental apparaus to enhance them reinforces the urban-rural divide in Chile and exacerbates the problems of ensuring social justice while pursuing economic growth through free-market philosophies.

308 **Urban transplantation in Chile.**
J. Douglas Porteous. *Geographical Review*, vol. 62, no. 4 (Oct. 1972), p. 455-78. maps.

A detailed research study of the closure of a copper mine in the central Andean region of Chile. The mine had its own town of workers and wives who were, with their families, re-located in large towns. The author discusses the reasons for the change, the programme of re-location and the reactions of the people involved. An interesting study in urban change.

309 **Monetary correction and housing finance in Colombia, Brazil and Chile.**
Roger James Sandilands. Farnborough, England: Gower, 1980. 492p. bibliog.

A valuable comparative study of the problems of the long-term financing of housing in inflationary situations, which argues that indexation would at least partly alleviate them, without causing distortions elsewhere.

Health

310 **Salud pública y bienestar social.** (Public health and social welfare.)
Edited by Mario Livingstone, Dagmar Raczynski.
Santiago: Universidad Católica de Chile, Centro de Estudios de Planificación Nacional, with the collaboration of the Institute of Development Studies, University of Sussex, 1976. 332p.

An outstanding collection of papers by leading authorities on this subject which, though dealing with the period prior to 1973 only, covers virtually every aspect of it to that time, such as structure of the health services, finance, access, infant mortality, nutrition and so on. Statistical tables and graphs substantiate the descriptions and commentaries.

311 **Development, reform, and malnutrition in Chile.**
Peter Hakim, Giorgio Solimano.   Cambridge, Massachusetts;
London: Massachusetts Institute of Technology Press, 1978. 91p.
bibliog. (International Nutrition Policy Series).
A well-researched study, backed up with numerous statistical tables, of the problem of malnutrition in Chile. The subject is treated historically, in this short, but important, study of a perennial problem.

312 **Food distribution and nutrition intervention: the case of Chile.**
Lloyd Harbert, Pasquale L. Scandizzo.   Washington, DC: World
Bank, 1982. 45p. bibliog. (Staff Working Papers, no. 512).
Governmental distribution of food to poor households began in 1924, though it has not been under a consistent programme or policy. The study considers the programme in the late 1970s, and uses data from a national nutritional survey of 1974-75.

313 **Health policy and social change: a comparative history of Chile and Cuba.**
Howard Waitzkin.   *Social Problems*, vol. 31, no. 2 (Dec. 1983),
p. 235-48. bibliog.
This article makes a comparative study of health care in the two countries, under their respective socialist régimes. The basic contrast is the comparatively reasonable level of care in Chile and the very low standard in Cuba when Castro came to power in 1959. The data on Chile is much better than that on Cuba, though the author argues that Cuba under Castro has fared better in this field than Chile under Allende.

314 **Free-market economic policies and infant and child mortality in Chile: multiple regression, principal components and simultaneous equation model results.**
David E. Hojman.   Liverpool: University of Liverpool, Centre
for Latin American Studies, 1985. 39p.
Despite the technicality of its title and some of its content, this is an interesting attempt to explain why, during the 1970s, when working-class living standards were falling, there was a marked decline in infant and child mortality rates. Part of the reason lies in the fact that high unemployment itself induces a decline in the birth-rate. The author suggests a number of specific policy measures to reduce infant mortality further.

Education

315 **Historia de la enseñanza en Chile.** (History of teaching in Chile.)
Amanda Labarca.   Santiago: Imprenta Universitaria, 1939. 399p.
bibliog.

Though published half a century ago, this still remains, for the Spanish-speaking reader, the best history of education in Chile down to the 1930s and the starting point for anyone interested in the subject.

316 **Philosophy and university reform at the University of Chile, 1842-1973.**
Iván Jaksíc.   *Latin American Research Review*, vol. 19, no. 1
(1984), p. 57-86.

An excellent survey of the evolution of philosophical thought and the study of philosophy in Chile, from the foundation of the national university to the University reforms of the late 1960s.

317 **Educational planning as political process: two case studies from Latin America.**
Noel McGinn, Ernesto Schiefelbein, Donald P. Warwick.
Comparative Education Review, vol. 23, no. 2 (June 1979),
p. 218-39.

A critical survey, using Chile and El Salvador as case studies, of the rationale of international aid-giving agencies in educational planning in Third World countries. Chile was one such country in the late 1960s, and the Chilean co-author of this article is an authority in the field. See also Harold Blakemore's 'Chile' in *Educational aid and national development* (q.v.).

318 **Chile.**
Harold Blakemore.   In: *Educational aid and national
development*. Edited by Nancy Parkinson. London; Basingstoke,
England: Macmillan, 1976, p. 330-68.

In this volume of studies of various countries, of the relationship between foreign assistance to education in the developing world and the growth of the recipient countries, the essay on Chile is useful. Written after the educational reforms of the Frei administration (1964-70), and based largely on field research, it summarizes what that government achieved and what role was played by external aid.

319 **Student politics in Chile.**
Frank Bonilla, Myron Glazer.   New York, London: Basic Books,
1970. 367p.

As in most Latin American countries, students in Chile have, in the modern period, been an influential minority pressure group in the nation's politics. This book, by two North American social scientists, based on field research, is an interesting study, concentrating on periods when the student body played an important, if not decisive, role in national life, notably in the 1920s-30s and the 1960s. A useful contribution which suggests that, although student politics may be eclipsed at times by authoritarian régimes, they cannot be ignored.

320 **The national unified school in Allende's Chile. The role of education in the destruction of a revolution.**
Joseph P. Farrell. Vancouver: University of British Columbia Press in association with the Centre for Research in Latin America and the Caribbean, York University, 1986. 263p. bibliog.
The national unified school was introduced by the Popular Unity government as a major reform of the secondary system. It aimed to make curricula more relevant to society. It became, however, an explosive political issue since the opposition saw it as a Marxist-inspired experiment. The author presents a convincing account of the subject and argues that the proposed reform was a major factor in the overthrow of Allende.

321 **Political ideology and educational reform in Chile, 1964-1976.**
Kathleen B. Fischer. Los Angeles: UCLA Latin American Center, 1979. 174p. bibliog.
An interesting comparative study of educational policies in Chile under the Christian Democrats in the 1960s, Popular Unity in the early 1970s, and the military régime since 1973. Its exploration of the ideologies behind the very different policies pursued is somewhat weak but the discussion of the policies themselves is very good.

322 **Eight years of their lives: through schooling to the labour market in Chile.**
Ernesto Schiefelbein, Joseph P. Farrell. Ottawa: International Development Research Centre, 1982. 207p.
Based on data collected from an initial sample of over 3,000 students, between 1970 and 1977, this study aims to identify the effects of different forms of education on people's futures. A meticulous piece of research, which also has some useful information on Chilean educational history.

323 **Educación y sociedad: Chile 1964-1984.** (Education and society: Chile 1964-1984.)
Guillermo Labarca. Amsterdam: Centre for Latin American Research and Documentation, 1985. 145p. (Latin America Studies, no. 32).
A critical analysis of educational developments in Chile from the Christian Democratic government (1964-70), through Popular Unity (1970-73) to the government of Pinochet (1973- ·) to 1984. Those two decades saw radical political change and valiant attempts by the first two governments to tackle Chile's educational problems. This has been reversed, in the author's view, by the

military government. The author, a supporter of Popular Unity, is also a well-known educationalist and his views must be taken seriously.

324 **Education and repression: Chile.**
Edited by Felicity Edholm.   London: World University Service, 1982. 79p. bibliog.
The political bias is obvious with regard to the educational changes under the Pinochet régime. However, this short work contains a good deal of information, presented in a lively manner.

325 **Changes in the Chilean educational system during eleven years of military government, 1973-1984.**
Ruth Aedo-Richmond, Inés Noguera, Mark Richmond.   In: *Education in Latin America*. Edited by Colin Brock, Hugh Lawlor. London: Croom Helm, 1985, p. 163-82.
A competent survey of the major educational changes in the specified period, concluding with the pessimistic but accurate assessment that, under the current régime, genuine improvement in educational provision is unlikely for most sectors of Chilean society.

326 **Chilean universities under the junta: régime and policy.**
Daniel C. Levy.   *Latin American Research Review*, vol. 21, no. 3 (1986), p. 95-128.
This article offers a critical survey, with detailed notes, of the military régime's attitudes and policies towards the higher education sector. The conclusions, that those policies are in accordance with an overall government strategy in terms of authoritarianism, are grave.

Labour and Unions

327 **Labour and politics in Chile.**
Alan Angell. In: *Latin American affairs. St. Antony's papers, no. 22.* Edited by Raymond Carr. Oxford: Oxford University Press, 1970, p. 107-35.

An elegantly written and neat summary of the evolution of the relationship between the Chilean labour movement and its political parties up to the mid-1960s. In one sense, it serves as an introduction to the author's more detailed study, but is an excellent starting point. See also *Politics and the labour movement in Chile* (q.v.).

328 **Politics and the labour movement in Chile.**
Alan Angell. London: Oxford University Press, 1972. 289p. map. bibliog.

This book is undoubtedly the best study in English of the Chilean working-class in terms of its growth, its unionization and its relations with political parties, from the late nineteenth century to the year of publication. Based on printed official sources and secondary works, it is enhanced by reports of personal interviews. It has, of course, been overtaken by events since 1973, but still stands as a major contribution to the understanding of both industrial relations in general and the trade union movement in particular.

329 **Elites, intellectuals and consensus: a study of the social question and the industrial relations system in Chile.**
James O. Morris. Ithaca, New York: Cornell University Press, 1966. 292p. bibliog. (Cornell International, Industrial and Labor Relations Reports, no. 7).

This once pioneering study, although now dated, remains a basic book for the understanding of both the social question in Chile and the development of the

82

industrial relations system from 1900 to just before the Second World War. Heavily-researched and based on a wide range of Chilean sources, it remains essential for the comprehension of the deep social divide in Chile which characterized the period and still remains.

330 **Labor in Latin America: comparative essays on Chile, Argentina, Venezuela and Colombia.**
Charles Bergquist.   Stanford, California: Stanford University Press, 1986. 397p.

A valuable cross-country study of those workers in the key sectors in each country who occupy a critical position in terms of production for export. The broad argument is that their bargaining power has been greater than has been thought, in terms of their influence on economic and political decision-making. This is certainly true of Chile, even under the present authoritarian régime.

331 **Land and labour in rural Chile, 1850-1935.**
Arnold Bauer, Ann Hagerman Johnson.   In: *Land and labour in Latin America. Essays on the development of agrarian capitalism in the nineteenth and twentieth centuries*. Edited by Kenneth Duncan, Ian Rutledge, with the collaboration of Colin Harding. Cambridge: Cambridge University Press, 1977, p. 83-102.

A short but perceptive essay, tracing the changes in land distribution in Chile during the period surveyed, and assessing the impact of these changes on rural labour.

332 **Political participation and rural labour in Chile.**
Brian Loveman.   In: *Political participation in Latin America*. Edited by John A. Booth, Mitchell A. Seligson. New York: Holmes & Meier, 1978, p. 183-97.

This is a valuable essay on rural labour patterns in the period between 1932 and 1973, emphasizing the encouragement given to promote rural unionization by the Christian Democratic government (1964-70) and the greater radicalization of the unions in the period 1970-73. The latter, however, led to a reaction among conservative land-owners, making, in the author's view, the military coup of 1973 almost inevitable. An excellent analysis by a leading authority on the subject of rural issues in Chile.

333 **Struggle in the countryside. Politics and rural labor in Chile, 1919-1973.**
Brian Loveman.   Bloomington, Indiana: Indiana University Press, 1976. 439p. 5 maps. bibliog. (International Development Research Center. Studies in Development, no. 10).

Based on field research in Chile in the early 1970s, this study is a detailed account of the Chilean land-holding system. It looks at the peasantry and their attempts to organize into unions. The period it covers ranges from the aftermath of the First World War, when the traditional systems of rural relationship were still largely

Labour and Unions

intact, to the Popular Unity government of Salvador Allende, when agrarian reform was greatly accelerated, only to be frustrated by the military coup of 1973. An important study with an excellent bibliography.

334 **The Valparaiso maritime strike of 1903 and the development of a revolutionary labor movement in Chile.**
Peter de Shazo. *Journal of Latin American Studies*, vol. 11, part 1 (May 1979), p. 145-68.

An extensively researched and important article on the growth of the Chilean labour movement. Taking the important strike in Valparaiso in 1903 as his case study, the author shows how it reflected growing left-wing class consciousness, the result of official repression and the failure to respond to workers' grievances. As a result of the strike, the unions retained a degree of independence from state control and became a significant political force in their own right.

335 **Urban workers and labor unions in Chile, 1902-1927.**
Peter de Shazo. Madison, Wisconsin; London: University of Wisconsin Press, 1983. 351p. bibliog.

The role of workers and unions in the evolution of modern Chile has been the subject of a substantial literature, to which this is a major recent contribution. Based on very detailed research and a comprehensive knowledge of the secondary sources, it challenges traditional assumptions about the alleged key position of the northern mining regions in working-class evolution, and places more emphasis on the urban workers, particularly of Santiago and Valparaiso. A most important study.

336 **The failure of populism in Chile: labour movement and politics before World War II.**
Jackie Roddick. *Boletín de Estudios Latinoamericanos y del Caribe*, no. 31 (Dec. 1981), p. 61-89. bibliog.

A thought-provoking article, analysing the evolution of the Chilean labour movement and emphasizing its distinctive political nature in Latin America. The writer argues that, compared with Argentina or Brazil, Chilean labour resisted populist policies and, thus, preserved its essentially genuine socialist nature. This is an important essay.

337 **Worker participation in company management in Chile: a historical experience.**
Manuel Barrera. Geneva: UN Research Institute for Social Development, 1981. 25p. bibliog. (Popular Participation Programme Occasional Paper. Report 81.3).

The popular participation programme of the Allende government was one of its most striking departures from traditional Chilean management methods. This is a very good description and evaluation of that programme.

338 **Economic democracy: workers' participation in Chilean industry, 1970-1973.**
Juan G. Espinosa, Andrew S. Zimbalist. New York: Academic Press, 1981. 211p. bibliog. (Studies in Social Discontinuity)

Although it is probably too heavily statistical for most readers, this study of the so-called 'social property sector' in Chile during the Allende period is useful. The book examines workers' participation in the period and takes a rather favourable view of its efficiency.

339 **El conflicto obrero en el enclave cuprífero chileno.** (Labour conflict in the Chilean copper enclave.)
Manuel Barrera. *Revista Mexicana de Sociología*, vol. 40, no. 2 (April-June 1978), p. 609-82.

A detailed study of labour relations in the vitally important copper mining sector of Chile, conducted prior to the implementation of the Pinochet government's trade union reforms. The author is a leading authority on the Chilean labour movement.

340 **Employment stagnation in Chile, 1974-1978.**
Patricio Meller, René Cortázar, Jorge Marshall. *Latin American Research Review*, vol. 16, no. 2 (1981), p. 144-55.

Though primarily of interest to economists, this article is not without value for others, as a discussion of the use of statistics by government. The official Chilean figures for employment in the country allege that, in the period surveyed, it grew by seven per cent, or approximately 200,000 new jobs, per year. The authors strongly refute this, arguing that the figures were distorted through over-reliance on material on Greater Santiago and neglect of provincial data, and supporting their contention with statistical data. Their conclusion is that employment stagnated nationally. Since the period surveyed was the first phase of the military government's restructuring of the economy, for which beneficial results were claimed, this is an important point to be raised, which certainly supports more impressionistic observations. Provides a valuable comment.

341 **Oral history and factory study: new approaches to labour history.**
Peter Winn. *Latin American Research Review*, vol. 14, no. 2 (1979), p. 130-40.

Based, in part, on his own study of the Yarur textile mill in Chile, the author argues for a greater concentration by labour historians on the lives of workers and their working conditions through the medium of oral history.

342 **Labour in Chile under the junta, 1973-1979.**
Gonzalo Falabella. London: University of London, Institute of Latin American Studies, [n.d.] 60p. (Working Papers, no. 4).

The military government in Chile, from 1973, embarked upon labour and union policies in sharp contrast to those found in Chilean history over the previous fifty years, which had seen a process of state accommodation with their demands. This careful study looks at those new policies in the first six years of authoritarian rule, emphasizing how new legislation attempted to curb union power and showing how working-class organizations responded to this.

343 **Nationalisation, copper miners and the military government in Chile.**
Francesco Zapata. In: *Miners and mining in the Americas*. Edited by Thomas Greaves, William Culver. Manchester: Manchester University Press, 1985, p. 256-76.

A short but interesting study of the copper miners' union at Chile's largest mine, Chuquicamata, showing how this 'aristocracy of labour' in the Chilean economy reacted to political events of the 1970s and 1980s. The author shows that, even under the repressive military government since 1973, the miners have retained their unity, largely because of their strategic position in the national economy.

344 **Participation. Trade unions and the state in present-day Chile.**
Manuel Barrera, Helia Henríques, Teresita Selamé.
Geneva: United Nations Research Institute for Social Development, 1986. 154p.

The most up-to-date survey and study of the Chilean trade unions under the military régime, which is based partly on interviews with union leaders and which puts the basic emphasis on collective bargaining. The team of writers are all members of the Centro de Estudios Sociales (Centre of Social Studies) in Santiago and the introduction is by the distinguished French Latin Americanist, Alain Touraine. A valuable contribution to the study of a key contemporary issue in Chile.

Government and Politics

General (to 1973)

345 **Legitimacy and stability in Latin America. A study of Chilean political culture.**
Francisco José Moreno.   New York: Praeger; London: University of London Press, 1969. 197p.

An interesting account of the evolution of the Chilean constitutional system, from the colonial period to the mid-1960s. The author's thesis is that Chilean stability, compared with most other Latin American states, derived less from democratization than from the popular appeal of traditional features such as respect for quasi-authoritarian leaders. Though it lacks a bibliography, the references are useful.

346 **The political system of Chile.**
Federico G. Gil.   Boston, Massachusetts: Houghton Mifflin Company, 1966. 323p. bibliog.

Written by a well-known Chilean political scientist, this first-rate introduction to the Chilean political system up to the mid-1960s still has considerable value for anyone wishing to understand how the Chilean democratic system worked.

347 **The timing, pace and sequence of political change in Chile, 1891-1925.**
Karen L. Remmer.   *Hispanic American Historical Review*, vol. 57, no. 2 (May 1977), p. 205-30.

The 'parliamentary period' in Chilean history (1891-1925) is usually regarded as one in which the dominant class played a purely political game, while social and economic issues were neglected. At the same time, however, it established a

87

number of democratic traditions which Chile enjoyed until 1973. This important article, in which the author surveys the political parties, how they operated, their social support and the drawbacks and advantages which the system entailed, concludes that Chile's democratic system emerged precisely because political power remained in few hands.

348 **Party competition in Argentina and Chile. Political recruitment and public policy, 1890-1930.**
Karen L. Remmer.   Lincoln, Nebraska; London: University of Nebraska Press, 1984. 296p. bibliog.

This is a valuable comparison of the political parties of Argentina and Chile, and their impact on public policy in a significant period for both countries. The sections on Chilean developments, like the rest, are carefully researched, and the author proves her thesis, which is that the élitist political system, with its emphasis on party competition, held back necessary social legislation. A number of detailed statistical tables, on such matters as the growth of the electorate, public expenditures, the occupational background of members of Congress and social legislation give added value to an important book.

349 **The Club de la Unión (Union Club) and kinship: social aspects of political obstructionism in the Chilean senate, 1920-1924.**
Gertrude Matyoka Yeager.   *The Americas*, vol. 35, no. 4 (April 1979), p. 539-72.

The Union Club in Santiago, founded in 1864, may be regarded as the physical expression of the close ties between members of the traditional Chilean aristocracy, whose interests appeared to be threatened by the social reformist policies of President Arturo Alessandri after his narrow electoral triumph in 1920. Those interests were represented politically by the Unionist party, and the author examines its compositon and activities in opposition to Alessandri. Although it is not entirely coherent in places, this is, nevertheless, a very useful addition to the study of kinship politics and of a key period in modern Chilean history.

350 **El movimiento popular chileno y el sistema de alianzas en la década de los treinta.** (The Chilean popular movement and the alliance system in the thirties.)
Hugo Zemelman.   In: *América Latina en los años treinta*. Co-ordinated by Pablo González Casanova. Mexico City: Universidad Nacional Autónoma, Instituto de Investigaciones Sociales, 1977, p. 378-450. bibliog. map.

An interesting Marxist analysis of Chile's political and economic history in a period when, for the first time, the left-wing parties, in alliance with the centrist Radical party, became a visible force on the Chilean political scene.

351 **The Chilean presidency in a developmental perspective.**
Jorge Tapia-Videla. *Inter-American Studies and World Affairs*,
vol. 19, no. 4 (Nov. 1977), p. 451-81.
A perceptive 'overview' by a leading Chilean political scientist of the country's
political and institutional evolution, which indicates why, in the author's view, the
tradition of consensus broke down in the 1970s.

352 **The politics of Chile: a sociogeographical assessment.**
César Caviedes L. Boulder, Colorado: Westview, 1979. 357p.
bibliog. (Westview Special Studies in Latin America).
A fascinating study by a geographer and geopolitician, which attempts to explain
the evolution of Chilean politics, from the 1950s to the date of publication, using
sociogeographical and quantitative techniques, notably on voting patterns. It is
important for its methodology as well as its content.

353 **Political participation, agriculture and literacy: communal versus
provincial voting patterns in Chile.**
Arturo Valenzuela. *Latin American Research Review*, vol. 12,
no. 1 (1977), p. 105-14.
A short, but provocative, article by a leading Chilean political scientist, resident
in the United States, suggesting that, in predominantly rural areas . . . urbanization is related more strongly to (political) participation, whereas in predominantly urban areas participation is more clearly associated with agricultural
activity'. He suggests that research at the communal level is likely to produce
more valid results than research at the provincial level.

354 **Political groups in Chile. The dialogue between order and change.**
Ben G. Burnett. Austin, Texas; London: University of Texas
Press for the Institute of Latin American Studies, 1970. 319p.
bibliog.
Written before the turbulent years of the Allende régime and the military
government which followed, this is still a useful survey, not only of Chilean
political parties at that time but also of other political actors, such as
management, labour, students and the military.

355 **The Chilean senate: internal distribution of influence.**
Weston H. Agor. Austin, Texas; London: University of Texas
Press for the Institute of Latin American Studies, 1971. 206p.
bibliog. (Latin American Monographs no. 23).
Though dated by the overthrow of constitutional rule in Chile from 1973, this is,
nonetheless, a useful study of how the traditional and democratic Chilean political
system worked. Based on field-work, it is a clinical analysis of the Chilean senate,
and helps to show why and how Chilean democracy worked, before it was
destroyed.

Government and Politics. General (to 1973)

356 **Authoritarianism and political culture in Argentina and Chile in the mid-1960s.**
Susan Tiano. *Latin American Research Review*, vol. 21, no. 1 (1986), p. 73-98.
Primarily of interest to political scientists, this well-documented essay in comparative politics investigates the relationship, in Argentina and Chile, between political structure and political culture. The jargon used could discourage the non-specialist reader.

357 **Corporatism and functionalism in modern Chilean politics.**
Paul W. Drake. *Journal of Latin American Studies*, vol. 10, no. 1, (May 1978), p. 83-116.
A valuable study, both of theories of corporatism and of that phenomenon in Chilean history. Corporatist ideas and organizations have played a significant part in modern Chilean development, and this well-documented essay has contemporary as well as historical relevance.

358 **Bureaucratic politics and administration in Chile.**
Peter S. Cleaves. Berkeley, California; Los Angeles: University of California Press, 1974. 352p. bibliog.
While this comparative study of Chilean administration relates essentially to the presidencies of Eduardo Frei (1964-70) and Salvador Allende (1970-73), it provides an excellent analysis of the Chilean bureaucracy and the making of policy when Chile was still a democratic state. Considerable attention is given to such aspects as planning, public works, housing and budgetary issues in this detailed study.

359 **Political brokers in Chile. Local government in a centralized polity.**
Arturo Valenzuela. Durham, North Carolina: Duke University Press, 1977. 272p. bibliog.
Traditionally, historians and social scientists concerned with Chile have seen that country's political and governmental system as being highly centralist in character. Little detailed research has hitherto been done on local government and its relations with both national political parties and central government. This very comprehensive study of such questions provides not only a corrective to much traditional thinking but is also an excellent piece of political science. The author concentrates on the modern period, prior to the military coup of 1973 which destroyed much of the municipal structure in Chile. However, he also glances backwards to the nineteenth century. An outstanding and essential book which illuminates better than any other, in English or Spanish, the relationship between central and local government in the democratic period.

360 **Chile: politics and society.**
Edited by Arturo Valenzuela, J. Samuel Valenzuela. New Brunswick, New Jersey: Transaction Books, 1976. 399p. bibliog.
A useful collection of essays by well-known writers on Chile, edited by a distinguished fraternity of Chilean social scientists. The emphasis is on the

Allende period and the essays, including contributions by the editors, range widely, covering such topics as labour, popular participation, the rural scene, political attitudes, US policy, and the role of foreign capital. It is to be commended, not least because of the different ideological standpoints of the authors.

361 **Chile: experiment in democracy.**
Sergio Bitar, translated from the Spanish by Sam Sherman.
Philadelphia: Institute for the Study of Human Issues, 1986. 243p.
(Inter-American Politics Series vol. 6).

The author is a well-known Chilean engineer and economist, who was closely involved with the policies of the socialist government of Salvador Allende. His book is not a polemic, but a careful and readable study of that period, with an introduction by the distinguished Brazilian scholar and economist, Celso Furtado.

362 **Search for justice: neighborhood courts in Allende's Chile.**
Jack Spence. Boulder, Colorado: Westview, 1979. 206p. bibliog.

One feature of Allende's 'Chilean road to socialism' was the setting-up of local tribunals, outside the framework of the existing legal system to try petty offences. This is a useful study of that attempt, though the author rather under-emphasizes the political dimension of the measure, which was a significant factor in the growth of opposition to Allende.

363 **The political mobilization of urban squatter settlements. Santiago's recent experience and its implications for urban research.**
Howard Handelman. *Latin American Research Review*, vol. 10, no. 2 (1975), p. 35-72.

Using Chilean experience of the mobilization and radicalization of squatter communities in Santiago, the author surveys the literature on such phenomena in a continental context. He also has much to say about the Chilean case when discussing the political attitudes of urban migrant settlements. The bibliography is comprehensive.

364 **Revolutionary social democracy: the Chilean Socialist party.**
Benny Pollack, Hernán Rosenkranz. London: Frances Pinter, 1986. 234p. bibliog.

Written by two members of the Chilean Socialist party of the former president, Salvador Allende, who are now both members of the British academic community, this is an important study, based to a large extent on party material. It is very well researched and annotated and is indispensable as an 'inside' view of the party's history and activities, particularly its organization prior to the military coup of 1973 and its response to the subsequent authoritarian rule. The fact that it is written from an ideological standpoint is obvious but not obtrusive.

365 **The Chilean Communist party and the road to socialism.**
Carmelo Furci. London: Zed Books, 1984. 204p. bibliog.

The author of this book, a member of the Italian Communist party and an academic, surveys the history of the Chilean Communist party which is one of the oldest in the world. He analyses its political strategies in considerable detail in this well-researched and important study.

366 Chile: a critical survey.
Edited by Tomás P. MacHale. Santiago: Institute of General Studies, 1972. 324p.

A useful collection of fifteen essays, written from the points of view of different disciplines, evaluating the Allende régime at mid-term. All the authors attack that régime, but this is not simply a right-wing tract, given the credentials of the writers.

367 Chilean's Chile.
Edited by K. Medhurst. *Government and Opposition*, vol. 7, no. 3 (summer 1972), p. 271-408.

A special issue of this well-known political science journal, devoted to Chile and containing six articles on the situation in Chile, as it was half-way through Allende's truncated term of office. It is a valuable commentary on how supporters and opponents of the socialist régime saw the position at that time.

368 Comandante Pepé.
Alistair Horne. *Encounter* (July 1971), p. 33-40.

A fascinating article on the Movement of the Revolutionary Left in southern Chile (the MIR), founded in the late 1960s. A fiercely ideological Marxist movement, it caused the Christian Democratic administration of Eduardo Frei, and that of his socialist successor, Salvador Allende, much trouble by its tactics of direct action. In fact, it was a major factor in causing the military to intervene in 1973. The author, a well-known English writer, interviewed Pepé, a leader of the MIR, in the first year of Allende's government (1971), before the MIR became impatient with his programme and resorted to extra-legal activities. A valuable piece of reporting, done at a critical moment in modern Chilean history.

369 Latin American military lore: an introduction and a case study.
Frederick M. Nunn. *The Americas*, vol. 35, no. 4 (1979), p. 429-74.

The leading authority on the Chilean military, who has also studied the institution in other Latin American and European countries, here gives us the benefit of his mastery of the subject and of his extensive knowledge of the literature. Taking Chile as his test case, he argues that the modern military in Latin America shares a body of professional thought and self-perception, transmitted from one generation of officers to the next. Based on both extensive study of the service publications and on oral interviews, this heavily-annotated article is essential reading for an understanding of the role of the military in Chilean development, especially in its latest phase.

370   **The new authoritarianism in Latin America.**
Edited by David Collier.   Princeton, New Jersey: Princeton
University Press for the Joint Committee on Latin American
Studies of the Social Science Research Council and the American
Council of Learned Societies, 1979. 456p. bibliog.

Although by the mid-1980s most of the military régimes in Latin America had
given way to civilian ones, this is a valuable dissection of the former by a number
of well-known specialists. Although it deals with the continent as a whole, the fact
that the Pinochet régime is only one of two still in power means that the essays on
Chile in this volume are relevant to the current situation.

371   **Armed forces of Latin America.**
Adrian J. English.   London: Jane's, 1984. 490p. maps. bibliog.

The section of this book which is devoted to Chile (p. 132-63) is a thorough and
detailed analysis of the current strength of the armed forces, their deployment
and material, which covers army, navy, naval aviation, air force and the para-
military police, or *carabineros*.

The Pinochet period (1973-   .)

372   **The revolution that never was: perspectives on democracy,
socialism, and reaction in Chile.**
Jorge Nef.   *Latin American Research Review*, vol. 18, no. 1
(1983), p. 228-45.

Written by a well-known Chilean political scientist and refugee from Pinochet's
Chile, this is a review article of nine studies on modern Chilean history, focusing
particularly on the Allende years (1970-73), the military coup of the latter year
and its aftermath. All the books reviewed are listed in this bibliography, with
comments, but this 'overview' is also worth listing for its insight into the events
described and evaluated in them.

373   **The crucial day, September 11, 1973.**
Augusto Pinochet Ugarte, translated by María Teresa Escobar.
Santiago: Editorial Renacimiento, 1982. 271p.

First published in Spanish in 1979 as the record of a long interview with Pinochet,
this is his account of how and why the services intervened in 1973. Its chief interet
lies in his *apologia* for that and subsequent events, indicating his ideology and
convictions. The large number of appendixes concerning the coup are also
interesting, though some readers may doubt their veracity.

Government and Politics. The Pinochet period (1973-   .)

374   **The murder of Chile: eyewitness accounts of the coup, the terror, and the resistance today.**
Samuel Chavkin.   New York: Everest House, 1982. 286p.

Based upon hundreds of interviews with Chilean exiles abroad, this is gripping testimony of the personal observations and experiences of those who have suffered under the Pinochet régime, particularly in its early years.

375   **Assassination on Embassy Row.**
John Dinges, Saul Landau.   New York: Pantheon, 1980. 411p.

An extremely detailed account of the successful plot to kill Orlando Letelier, a key opponent of Pinochet, and his secretary, Ronni Moffitt, of the assassination itself and what followed that event in 1976. Both Letelier and Mrs Moffit's husband worked at the Institute for Policy Studies and this book was written under its aegis. It is still, however, a highly convincing story.

376   **New thoughts on military intervention in Latin American politics: the Chilean case.**
Frederick M. Nunn.   *Journal of Latin American Studies*, vol. 7, part 2 (Nov. 1975), p. 271-304.

An important article, taking as its point of departure the military coup of 1973, but also reflecting on the continuities in Chilean military thought and the relationship between the services and the civil power. It also contains theoretical implications for the study of the military in Latin America in general.

377   **Military rule in Chile: dictatorships and oppositions.**
Edited by J. Samuel Valenzuela, Arturo Valenzuela.   Baltimore, Maryland; London: Johns Hopkins University Press, 1986. 331p.

The result of a workshop on 'six years of military rule in Chile', held at the Woodrow Wilson Center in Washington, DC in May 1980, this series of essays on Chile under President Pinochet is an excellent collection relating to near-contemporary Chilean history and politics. The participants were mostly academics, and the papers presented in this volume on economic, political, social and international aspects of the post-Allende government are well-researched and constructive. This is probably the best one-volume survey of Chile from 1973 to the early 1980s in print.

378   **Military dictatorship and political opposition in Chile, 1973-86.**
Brian Loveman.   *Journal of Inter-American Studies and World Affairs*, vol. 28, no. 3 (Winter, 1986-67), p. 1-38. bibliog.

A succinct and perceptive analysis of political developments in Chile since the military coup of 1973.

379   **The role of military expenditure in the development process: Chile,
1952-1973, and 1973-1980; two contrasting cases.**
Carlos Portales, Augusto Veras.   *Ibero-Americana*, vol. 12,
nos. 1-2 (1983), p. 21-50.
A major investigation of the allocation of public expenditures in the two periods,
with the emphasis on military spending on which the tables are revealing.
Although the article might seem to be primarily for economists, it substantiates,
in fact, the view that the treatment of the military in the earlier period was a
factor in their overthrow of civilian government in 1973, and that the cohesion of
the services since then has depended, in part, on more generous treatment by
government.

380   **Chile: the Pinochet decade. The rise and fall of the Chicago boys.**
Phil O'Brien, Jackie Roddick.   London: Latin America Bureau
(Research & Action). 1983. 118p. map.
A strongly-worded attack on the policies pursued in Chile between 1973, when
the military took power, and 1983 when the economic model seemed to have
collapsed. Though somewhat polemic in tone, it is worth reading as a left-wing
interpretation.

381   **Chile after 1973: elements for the analysis of military rule.**
Edited by David E. Hojman.   Liverpool: Centre for Latin
American Studies, University of Liverpool, 1985. 152p.
(Monograph Series, no. 12).
A useful collection of essays on Chile under the Pinochet régime. Topics covered,
by various people, are economic policies, agrarian developments, the Church, the
external debt and the new song movement. The concluding essay by the editor is
an econometric analysis concentrating on the fixed exchange rate policy of 1979-
82. All the entries are highly critical of the Pinochet government.

382   **Economic liberalism and political repression in Chile.**
Jorge Nef.   In: *Latin American Prospects for the 1980s: equity,
democratization and development*. Edited by Archibald R. M.
Ritter, David H. Pollock. New York: Praeger, 1983, p. 304-29.
Written by a reputable Chilean political scientist, in exile in Canada, this is a
short but valuable analysis of the factors which led to military intervention in
1973, and the establishment and consolidation of the Pinochet régime. It is not
entirely up-to-date, of course, but it provides a reliable dissection of the various
forces which support or oppose that régime.

383   **Chile since the coup: ten years of repression.**
C. G. Brown.   New York: Americas Watch, 1983. 137p. bibliog.
(An Americas Watch Report).
A well-constructed discussion of the abuses of political, individual and cultural
human rights in Pinochet's Chile. It also details the involvement of the United

States in the fall of Allende. This is depressing but necessary reading for the period.

384   **Chileans in exile. Private struggles, public lives.**
Diana Kay.   Basingstoke, England: Macmillan, 1987. 225p.
bibliog. (Edinburgh Studies in Sociology).

This is the most detailed account of the Chilean diaspora after the coup of 1973. The writer relies heavily on personal interviews, giving the book its immediacy. Written from a feminist standpoint, it is a valuable study which also includes a useful statistical table of the destinations of the 26,000 or so refugees.

385   **The exile question in Chilean politics.**
Alan Angell, Susan Carstairs.   *Third World Quarterly*, vol. 9, no. 1 (Jan. 1987), p. 148-67.

An interesting and useful survey of Chilean refugees from the Pinochet régime and of how that government has used the exiles as an instrument of political coercion. It considers who the exiles are, their current locations and the differential impact of the experience on the various political parties.

386   **Torture in Chile.**
London: Amnesty International, 1983. 72p.

An Amnesty International team visited Chile in April and May of 1982, to investigate the situation regarding human rights. The report is a graphic and horrifying account, based on medical evidence and other testimony, of how torture has been used in Chile as an instrument of state control.

387   **Report on the situation of human rights in Chile.**
Washington, DC: Organization of American States, General Secretariat, 1985. 336p.

This report, a lengthy indictment of the Pinochet régime's record on human rights, covers the period from the coup of 1973 to 1984.

388   **Back to the barracks: the Chilean case.**
Harold Blakemore.   *Third World Quarterly*, vol. 7, no. 1 (Jan. 1985), p. 44-62.

Against the historical background of the Chilean armed services and politics, the author discusses the situation of President Pinochet to the time of writing, and suggests possible scenarios for the return of the military to the barracks.

Economy

General

389 **Monetary and banking policy of Chile.**
Guillermo Subercaseaux.   Oxford: Clarendon, 1922. 217p.
Although it is obviously not relevant to the modern period, this book, by a
professor of economics at the University of Chile, is still valuable. It is the nearest
thing to an English-language history of banking in Chile down to the date of
publication, and much of the historical data has not yet been superseded.

390 **The growth and structure of the Chilean economy: from
independence to Allende.**
Markos J. Mamalakis.   New Haven, Connecticut; London: Yale
University Press, 1976. 390p.
Written by a leading authority on Chilean economics and economic history, this
detailed and heavily statistical account of the development of the Chilean
economy concentrates on the period since 1930 and, in that respect, is the nearest
thing in English to a single volume economic history of Chile to 1970. Though
written largely from the standpoint of an academic economist, with an unrivalled
knowledge of Chilean statistical sources, it is indispensable reading for anyone
interested in the country in general.

391 **Origins of the politics of inflation in Chile, 1888-1918.**
Thomas C. Wright.   *Hispanic American Historical Review*,
vol. 53, no. 2 (May 1973), p. 239-59.
A well-researched and interesting article, focusing on the growth of the popular
reaction to the growth of inflation in Chile, arising from the inflationary effects of
taxes on cattle imports, imposed by the landed aristocracy. The author illustrates
clearly the importance of this factor in shaping the political attitudes and
developing the consciousness of the working-class.

97

392 **Journeys toward progress. Studies of economic policy-making in Latin America.**
Albert O. Hirschman.   New York: Twentieth Century Fund, 1963. 308p.

The chapter on inflation in Chile (p. 161-223) in this collection of economic essays is a masterly discussion of that perennial problem in the country's history, which, despite the date of publication, still remains relevant.

393 **Industrial development in a traditional society: the conflict of entrepreneurship and modernization in Chile.**
Henry W. Kirsch.   Gainesville, Florida: University Presses of Florida, 1977. 210p. bibliog.

The author investigates the much discussed question of why Chile, with considerable natural resources and a comparatively well-educated people, failed to become a truly industrial nation, especially during a key period of modern history, between the late 1870s and 1930. His answer lies in the particular structure of Chilean society, notably its hierarchic nature and the dominance of a small economic élite. Well-researched and competently argued, this is a valuable study.

394 **Chile: an economy in transition.**
P. T. Ellsworth.   New York: Macmillan, 1945. 183p. map.

Despite its age, this book is still the most complete study of the impact of the world depression (1929-32) on the Chilean economy and of the measures taken during the 1930s and early 1940s to aid recovery from it. It is replete with statistical data and is essential for the understanding of the Chilean economy in a drastic period of transition.

395 **Essays on the Chilean economy.**
Markos Mamalakis, Clark Winton Reynolds.   Homewood, Illinois: Richard D. Irwin, 1965. 409p. bibliog.

This important study consists of two large essays. The first, by Mamalakis, considers public policy and sectoral development in the Chilean economy between 1940 and 1958; the second, by Reynolds, looks at the development problems of an export economy, taking Chile and copper as the themes of the thesis. These two essays which have been researched closely are essential reading for an understanding of the Chilean economy for this period. Both are well supported by statistical tables.

396 **Contribution of copper to Chilean economic development, 1920-67: profile of a foreign-owned export sector.**
Markos Mamalakis.   In: *Foreign investment in the petroleum and mineral industries*. Edited by Raymond F. Mikesell and associates. Baltimore, Maryland: Johns Hopkins University Press, 1971, p. 387-420.

A succinct analysis of the contribution of large-scale copper mining to Chile's economic growth. The author is the leading authority on the Chilean economy.

397 **Multinational corporations and the politics of dependence. Copper in Chile.**
Theodore H. Moran. Princeton, New Jersey: Princeton University Press, 1975. 286p. bibliog.

This is a very detailed study of the relationship between the multinational corporations which controlled the Chilean copper industry until nationalization in the early 1970s and the host government. In one sense, it is a study of conflict, with valuable information for other case studies. Moran details the process, from 1945 to the early 1970s, of the erosion by successive Chilean governments of the monopolistic control of Chile's basic natural resource by foreign corporations, which culminated in outright take-over in 1971. In another sense, therefore, it is a study of Chilean economic nationalism, and is an important book.

398 **Inflation in developing countries: an econometric study in Chilean inflation.**
Vittorio Corbo Lioi. Amsterdam: North-Holland, 1974. 286p. bibliog.

Inflation has been virtually endemic in Chile since the late 1870s, when an economic crisis pushed the government to abandon the metallic standard. This is a meticulous, highly specialized work, for economists, using a macroeconomic model to consider the results of inflation and particularly how it affects policy decisions, and also to suggest some. Despite political and economic changes since it appeared, its analysis is still relevant.

399 **Foreign trade regimes and economic development in Chile.**
Jere R. Behrman. New York: National Bureau of Economic Research, 1976. 408p. (Special Conference Series on Foreign Trade Regimes and Economic Development).

Essentially a book for the academic or professional economist, this is a highly technical analysis of the various factors affecting Chilean trade flows, up to the date of publication. It deals with all aspects of the subject – government policies, including attempts at trade liberalization as opposed to a traditional protective tariff structure, in the 1960s and 1970s, costs, exchange rates, merchandise exports and balance of payments problems. It is a clinical study.

400 **Allende's Chile. The political economy of the rise and fall of the Unidad Popular.**
Stefan de Vylder. Cambridge: Cambridge University Press, 1976. 251p. bibliog. (Cambridge Latin American Studies, no. 25).

First published in Sweden in 1974, this book, which is based largely on the author's research in Chile in 1972 and 1973, is a very good examination of the economic policies, problems and progress of the Marxist government of Salvador Allende. The author does not hide his sympathies with that government and its professed aims, but neither is he uncritical of what he regards as its mistakes. An excellent study, which is marred only by the lack of an index.

401 **Income redistribution in Chile, 1970-73.**
Astrig Tasgian. Turin: Tirrenia-Stampatori, 1983. 161p. bibliog.
A very useful study, replete with tables, of a critical part of the economic policy of the Allende government, it also has theoretical implications for those interested in development in general.

402 **Chilean economic policy.**
Edited by Juan Carlos Méndez. Santiago: Imprenta Calderón y Cía, 1979. 386p.
This is now somewhat dated. However, it is still probably the best statement, in English, of the economic aims, programmes and policies of the Pinochet régime, consisting largely of public statements made by prominent government spokesmen from Pinochet down. This valuable historical record contains a large number of statistical tables. The fluctuations affecting the Chilean economy since the book appeared have not essentially changed the government's basic economic philosophy.

403 **Chile, an economy in transition.**
Washington, DC: Latin America & the Caribbean Regional Office, World Bank, 1980. 584p. bibliog. (A World Bank Country Study).
This is unrivalled as the most comprehensive survey of the Chilean economy in the first years of the Pinochet government, with valuable material also on the period from 1964 to 1973, backed up with extensive statistical tables.

404 **Mapa de la extrema riqueza: los grupos económicos y el proceso de concentración de capitales.** (Map of extreme wealth: economic groups and the capital concentration process.)
Fernando Dahse. Santiago: Editorial Aconcagua, 1979. 209p.
This is a detailed analysis of the major economic groups in Chile after the first phase of the Pinochet economic 'reconstruction'. Though somewhat dated, it is still valuable.

405 **Adjusting taxation of business income for inflation: lessons from Brazil and Chile.**
Keith S. Rosenn. *Texas International Law Journal*, vol. 13, no. 2 (spring 1978), p. 165-97.
Primarily of interest to economists, this is a detailed cross-country study of the effects of tax indexation based on the experiences of Brazil and Chile, where similar policies were pursued in the 1970s.

Economy. General

406   The political economy of repressive monetarism: the state and
      capital accumulation in post-1973 Chile.
      Carlos Fortín.   In: *The state and capital accumulation in Latin
      America. Vol. 1. Brazil, Chile, Mexico.* Edited by Christian
      Anglade, Carlos Fortín. London; Basingstoke, England:
      Macmillan, 1985, p. 139-209. bibliog.
A highly critical survey of Chilean economic policies under Pinochet, by a former
member of Salvador Allende's government who has been in exile since Pinochet
came to power. A large number of statistical tables buttress a well-argued
critique.

407   Recent development of the securities market in Chile.
      Santiago: Superintendencia de Valores y Seguros, 1982. 68p.
      bibliog.
Although it was written before the financial crisis that hit the Chilean economy
early in 1983, this is a useful and accurate guide to the Chilean stock-market,
before that date.

408   Recent southern cone liberalization reforms and stabilization
      policies: the Chilean case, 1974-1982
      Roberto Zahler.   *Journal of Inter-American Studies and World
      Affairs*, vol. 25, no. 4 (Nov. 1983), p. 509-62. bibliog.
Statistical tables support this fairly factual, careful and useful survey of Chile's
economic progress, from the coup of 1973 to the beginnings of the severe
economic depression of the early 1980s. It is recommended for those who do not
wish to survey the monograph literature, which is now very extensive on this
subject.

409   Chile.
      In: *South American economic handbook*. Edited by Harold
      Blakemore. London: Euromonitor Publications, 1986, p. 95-111.
      map.
A succinct account of the Chilean economy, from 1973 to the mid-1980s, giving
the basic facts, with statistical tables, of the different sectors.

410   Neoconservative economics in the southern cone of Latin America,
      1973-1983.
      Joseph Ramos.   Baltimore, Maryland; London: Johns Hopkins
      University Press, 1986. 200p. bibliog.
This is the best and the most up-to-date survey of the liberal economic policies
pursued by Argentina, Chile and Uruguay in this decade, when all three countries
were under military rule and adopted 'free-market' policies. There is a large
amount of recondite material on Chile throughout the book, and the bibliography
is excellent. The author's view, in summary, is that the 'free-market' policy failed
to generate development. While he does not hide his own prescriptions, he is
admirably objective.

101

Business and industry

411 **An analysis of the financial and investment activities of the Chilean
development corporation, 1939-1974.**
Markos Mamalakis. *Journal of Development Studies*, vol. 5, no. 2
(Jan. 1969), p. 118-37.

The Chilean Development Corporation (CORFO) was established in 1939, in the
wake of a devastating earthquake in the south. It was the first Latin American
general development and economic planning authority, and had wide powers to
promote growth. The corporation also played a major part in the expansion of the
role of the state in the economy, promoting such entities as the National
Petroleum Corporation, the National Electricity Board, the Steel Company of the
Pacific, and many others. This is a useful survey of its investment policies up to
the advent of the *laissez-faire* Pinochet government.

412 **Manufacturing in the Concepción region of Chile: present position
and prospects for future development.**
J. H. Butler. Washington, DC: National Academy of Sciences
and National Research Council, 1960. 106p. maps.

A useful study in historical geography and regional development, this book
describes and discusses how the city of Concepción, at the southern end of Chile's
central valley, developed an industrial-manufacturing base, with a wide range of
products. Until the present decade it looked to become a desirable alternative
growth-pole, to challenge the dominance of the Santiago-Valparaiso axis.
However, current economic policies have somewhat reduced that possibility.

413 **The comparative management of firms in Chile.**
Bernard D. Estafen. Bloomington, Indiana: Foundation for the
School of Business, Indiana University, 1973. 217p. bibliog.
(International Business Research Series, no. 4).

This is a detailed study of business organization in Chile, before the coup of 1973.
The author compares and contrasts the operations of American-owned enterprises
in Chile with domestic companies, covering almost all aspects of their
performance, such as strategies, markets, staffing, labour force and profitability.
It is replete with statistics. Although changes in economic policy since its
publication have dated some of the data, much of what the author says is still
highly relevant, not least with the return of American capital to Chile in the post-
Allende years and the survival through the recession of the early 1980s of many
large Chilean companies.

414 **A model of the small Chilean firm.**
Michael B. Anderson. Ithaca, New York: Cornell University,
Latin American Studies Program, 1972. 155p. bibliog.
(Dissertation Series, no. 38).

Though based on field research undertaken in the late 1960s, this is still a useful study of small-scale Chilean business, with useful theoretical consideration of the development of that type of enterprise.

415 **Expropriation of U.S. property in South America. Nationalization of oil and copper companies in Peru, Bolivia and Chile.**
George M. Ingram. New York: Praeger, 1974. 392p.

About a quarter of this book is devoted to the Chilean experience, with the subject being treated in historical perspective. The emphasis is, inevitably, on copper, but the author's general propositions and conclusions merit attention. This is a very useful study of the relationship between multinational companies and successive Chilean governments, over the disposal of the state's major economic asset.

416 **Expropriation of U.S. investments in Cuba, Mexico and Chile.**
Eric N. Baklanoff. New York: Praeger, 1975. 170p.

A comparative study of the experiences of three Latin American countries with nationalization. The section devoted to Chile is essentially concerned with the state take-over, under the government of Popular Unity, of the large copper mining interests owned, to a great extent, by United States' interests.

417 **Dependent industrialisation in Latin America.**
Rhys Owen Jenkins. New York: Praeger; London: Martin Robertson, 1977. 298p.

This is a clinical study of the development of the automobile industry in Argentina, Chile and Mexico, valuable for the study of Chile because of the absence of other works in English on the subject. Well-researched and closely-argued, it includes consideration of the attempt made under the Popular Unity government (1970-73) to restructure the industry. The approach, however, is somewhat narrowly economic.

418 **Industrial development in the periphery: the motor vehicle industry in Chile.**
Robert N. Gwynne. *Bulletin of the Society for Latin American Studies*, no. 29 (Nov. 1978), p. 47-69. map.

A highly competent discussion of the policies of various governments towards the vehicle industry, and its location and development. The author contrasts the previous attempt (under Allende) to decentralize industry which involved placing the major assembly plants away from the central region, a policy reversed by the Pinochet government, much to the author's critical regret.

419 **The deindustrialization of Chile, 1974-1984.**
R. N. Gwynne. *Bulletin of Latin American Resarch*, vol. 5, no. 1 (1986), p. 1-23.

An important article, tracing the impact of the economic policies of the Pinochet régime on Chilean industry. The author concludes that the 'free-market' policy, emphasizing external competition in the industrial sector and primary exports, has had deleterious effects on employment, investment and Chile's capacity for a significant increase in international trade.

420   **Import substitution and the decentralisation of industry in less developed countries: the television industry in Chile, 1962-74.**
R. N. Gwynne.   Birmingham, England: University of Birmingham, Department of Geography, 1980. 30p. (Occasional Publication no. 12).

An interesting case study of changing government policies and their impact both on local industry and employment. The author, a leading authority on the regional and industrial development of Chile, traces the fortunes of the television industry in the free port of Arica, from the socialist régime of Allende to the free-enterprise model of the military junta. He measures the effect of the latter's unwillingness to protect domestic industry, which has led to higher unemployment.

421   **Deindustrialisation in Chile.**
Jaime Gatica Barros.   Boulder, Colorado: Westview, 1987. 120p.

A survey and investigation of the impact on national industry of the free-market economic policies pursued by the Pinochet government. The conclusions are pessimistic.

Transport

422   **South American packets. The British packet service to Brazil, the River Plate, the west coast (via the Straits of Magellan) and the Falkland Islands, 1808-1880.**
J. N. T. Howat.   York, England: Postal History Society in association with William Sassons, 1984. 283p.

A fascinating study of the British packet-boat service to South America in the nineteenth century, in which one chapter is devoted to the service of steamships established by the Pacific Steam Navigation Company, to travel to Chile through the Straits of Magellan, in 1868. An important and well-illustrated contribution to South American postal history. See also *The Pacific Steam Navigation Company. Its maritime postal history, 1840-1853, with particular reference to Chile* (q.v.).

423   **The Pacific Steam Navigation Company. Its maritime postal history, 1840-1853, with particular reference to Chile.**
A. R. Doublet.   London: Royal Philatelic Society, 1983. 70p.

The Pacific Steam Navigation Company (PSNC) was founded in Liverpool on the initiative of the North American engineer William Wheelwright in 1840, to connect the Pacific ports of South America with western Europe. In 1842 it signed a postal agreement with the Chilean government for the transport of mail. This is an interesting study of that relationship to 1853 when the Chilean postal service began. Valuable, not least for its illustrations, to all philatelists.

424 **Chile's central valley railroads and economic development in the nineteenth century.**
Robert Oppenheimer. *Proceedings of the Pacific Coast Council on Latin American Studies*, no. 6 (1977-79), p. 73-86.
Really an essay in transport history, this is a seriously-researched study of the establishment and growth of the Chilean railways in the core region of the country and their contribution to economic development.

425 **Railways of South America. Part III. Chile.**
W. Rodney Long. Washington, DC: Government Printing Office for the US Department of Commerce, 1930. 373p. maps. (Trade Promotion Series, no. 93).
A most exhaustive survey of the Chilean railway system, public and private, covering the period up the late 1920s. It deals with the railways' history, describes their condition, workings, management and labour, traffic, tariffs and profits at that time. There are a large number of statistical appendixes. Although it was written long before such modern technological improvements as electrification, the book is quite indispensable as a reference work on the historical growth and evolution of Chilean railways.

426 **Railways of the Andes.**
Brian Fawcett. London: George Allen & Unwin, 1963. 328p. bibliog. 6 maps.
An excellent and readable account of the building and operation of the major railways traversing the Andean mountain chain, including Chilean railways such as the Antofagasta (Chili) and Bolivia Railway Co. Ltd., and the transandine railroad links with Argentina. Highly recommended, and not only to railway enthusiasts.

427 **Les transports en commun à Santiago du Chili: problèmes et perspectives.** (Public transport in Santiago, Chile: problems and perspectives.)
Jacques Santiago. *Cahiers d'Outre-Mer*, vol. 31, no. 122 (1978), p. 152-70.
Approximately ninety per cent of the population of Chile's capital depends on public transport. This is a detailed investigation of the system, with particular emphasis on the underground, which was started in 1969. A highly informative article on a little-studied subject, and one of great significance considering the fact that about one third of all Chileans live in the metropolis.

428 **Geografía de transporte y comunicaciones.** (Geography of transport
and communications.)
O. Muñiz.   Santiago: Instituto Geográfico Militar, *Colección
Geografía de Chile*, vol. 13, 1985. 198p.
The most recent and detailed survey of the Chilean transport and communications
system, including seven photographs, fifty-seven figures and thirty-eight tables.

429 **Airlines of Latin America since 1919.**
R. E. G. Davies.   London: Putnam, 1984. 698p. maps.
The section on Chile (p. 523-42), in this lavishly illustrated and highly detailed
account of the growth of Latin America's airlines, is the best short account in
English. It traces the evolution of the Chilean companies, both public and private,
from the pioneering flights of such national heroes as Arturo Merino Benítez, the
first man to fly across the Antarctic, in the late 1920s, to the present day.
Santiago's international airport, formerly named Pudahuel, was renamed in his
honour by the present military government.

Minerals and mining

430 **Mining Annual Review.**
London: Mining Journal. 1935- . annual
Chile has enormous wealth and potential in mineral resources, such as copper,
gold, molybdenum, silver, lithium, coal, nitrates and other salts. This is an
indispensable up-dated source of information on Chilean mining, with reports too
numerous to enunerate. For example the *Mining Magazine*, a periodical offshoot
of the parent company, published in November 1986 a special issue on mining in
Latin America, which contained a lot of recondite material on Chile, including
statistics, technical information and geographical data.

431 **Minerals Yearbook.**
Washington, DC: Government Printing Office. 1932/33- . 3 vols.
annual.
The third volume of this indispensable reference work is entitled *Area Reports
International* and, inevitably, includes Chile. It covers all the economic
factors – output, exports, imports, projects and the respective exploration
activities undertaken by both government and private investors.

432 **The mining industry of the Norte Chico, Chile.**
Leland R. Pederson.   Evanston, Illinois, 1966. 305p. 13 maps.
bibliog. (Northwestern University Studies in Geography. no. 11.)
This is a meticulously researched study of the evolution of the mining industry of
the northern Chilean provinces of Atacama and Coquimbo, from the colonial
period to the date of publication. It emphasizes the continuity of the mining

tradition in the region – gold, silver and copper – and is an outstanding contribution, not only to the study of Chile's regional geography but also to its economic history.

433 **El cobre chileno.** (Chilean copper.)
Prepared by a group of specialists under the direction of Andrés Zauschquevich, Alexander Sutulov. Santiago: Editorial Universitaria, 1975. 520p.

An immensely detailed work on Chile's major natural resource, covering the history of copper and the evolution of the industry, with detailed descriptions of the major mines and of the smaller enterprises, investment, commerce, and industrial relations. In short, it is a comprehensive survey, embellished with numerous plates and statistical tables.

434 **The decline of the copper industry in Chile and the entrance of north American capital.**
Joanne Fox Przeworski. New York: Arno, 1980. 323p. bibliog.
(Arno Press Collection on Multinational Corporations: Operations and Finance).

Adapted from the author's doctoral dissertation of Washington University (1978), this is a well-researched study of the process whereby Chilean interests in copper were replaced by the large-scale mines under North American control in the first half of this century.

435 **Chile. Nuestro cobre.** (Chile. Our copper.)
Jorge Alvear Urrutia. Santiago: Editores Lastra, SA, 1974. 211p. 2 maps.

A beautifully produced survey of what is known as the *Gran Minería* (large-scale mining) of copper in Chile, containing a history and description of the huge enterprises such as Chuquicamata, El Teniente, El Salvador, Minas Blancas and Potrerillos, which are located mostly in the northern desert. The author also covers the social life of the mining communities, as well as other aspects of the mainstay of the Chilean economy. The non-Spanish reader may not cope with the text, but would be considerably compensated by the large number of magnificent colour photographs which accompany it.

436 **Anaconda.**
Isaac F. Marcosson. New York: Dodd, Mead, 1957. 370p.

The Anaconda Company, an American Corporation, is the largest non-ferrous mining and metal making organization in the world, especially in copper. Until its Chilean properties were nationalized in 1971, it owned Chuquicamata, on the Andean slopes in northern Chile, which is not only the largest open-cast mine in the world but also the one with the biggest copper reserves. Chapter Nine of this history of the corporation (p. 194-219) is a highly readable account of its Chilean properties and operations up to the mid-1950s.

437 **Braden: historia de una mina.** (Braden: the history of a mine.)
Luis Hiriart. Santiago: Editorial Andes, 1964. 312p.

A highly eulogistic account of the American mining engineer, William Braden, and his exploits in Chile. He first arrived there in 1894 and ten years later he acquired the massive copper mountain of El Teniente, about one hundred miles south-east of Santiago, which was Chile's first large-scale mining venture. Though the Braden Copper Company sold out a few years later, Braden had laid the foundations and provided the infrastructure of one of the most fabulous mines in the history of copper. A useful account, though perhaps too favourable to the Company when considering its dealings with the workers.

438 **The Kennecott white paper on Chile's expropriation of El Teniente copper mine.**
Kennecott Copper Corporation. *Inter-American Economic Affairs*, no. 25 (1972), p. 25-38.

In 1971, prior to the nationalization of the Chilean copper mines and the expropriation of the mainly American-owned large mines, the Allende government passed a law enabling it to take over El Teniente, without compensation. This is the company's case against that law, alleging violation of international law and practice.

439 **Chile: where major new copper output can materialize faster than anywhere else.**
Engineering and Mining Journal, no. 180 (1979), p. 68-111.

A general but well-illustrated survey of the major Chilean copper mines, and an assessment of future ore grade prospects and profitability. This is a useful review of the larger copper mines in the country which are estimated to hold about one-third of the world's entire copper reserves.

440 **Mantos Blancos.**
Mining Magazine (Dec. 1981), p. 458-69.

This anonymous article, based on a visit to the mine and on information supplied by its management, is an excellent case study of one of Chile's major copper mines, describing the geological environment and technical details of its operation. The mine is situated in the Atacama desert, about forty-five kilometres north-east of the city of Antofagasta, northern Chile's major urban centre and chief port.

441 **Codelco's development plans for Chuquicamata and El Teniente.**
Ronald D. Crozier. *Mining Magazine* (Nov. 1986), p. 460-69. map.

Chile possesses about one-third of the world's known copper reserves and, in Chuquicamata, has the largest open mine in the world. El Teniente is one of the biggest underground mines. This article is an excellent survey of the expansion plans of the Chilean copper corporation (CODELCO) into the 1990s.

442   **Iron ore fields of the world. II. El Algarrobo of Chile.**
      Metal Bulletin, 9 October, 1962, p. 1-4 map.

Situated some thirty-five kilometres south-west of the town of Vallenar, in the
semi-arid zone of northern Chile, the El Algarrobo open-cast iron-ore mine is
Chile's largest exploited deposit, with an estimated seventy million tonnes of
reserves. This short, illustrated descriptive article is now somewhat dated, but it
does provide a useful geological, historical and technical account.

443   **The small mining industry in Chile.**
      Hector Marinovic Olivos.   In: *Small scale mining of the world.*
      New York: United Nations Institute for Training and Research,
      1978, p. 529-42.

A paper given at a specialist conference in Mexico, this is a critical study of the
operations of ENAMI, the Chilean state corporation charged with encouraging
small-scale mining. The author argues that its success has been limited and
suggests ways for improvement.

444   **Gold mining in Chile.**
      Ronald D. Crozier.   *Mining Magazine* (May 1984), p. 460-61.

Though very short, this is a useful summary of gold mining in Chile. A short
historical introduction is followed by a survey of the current situation, highlighting
the growth in output in recent years and the encouraging outlook for the future.

445   **History of the Chile nitrate industry.**
      M. B. Donald.   *Annals of Science*, vol. 1, no. 1 (Jan. 1936),
      p. 29-47; no. 2 (April 1936), p. 193-216.

Most of the vast literature on nitrates is in Spanish but these two articles provide
an excellent short account in English, of both historical and technical interest.

446   **Chilean nitrate mining.**
      Ronald D. Crozier.   *Mining Magazine* (Sept. 1981), p. 160-73.
      map.

A succinct summary of the modern Chilean nitrate industry, with the emphasis on
its technical evolution and current operations.

Fishing, agriculture and forestry

447   **Geografía del mar chileno.** (Geography of the Chilean sea.)
      José R. Canón, E. Morales.   Santiago: Instituto Geográfico
      Militar, *Collección Geografía de Chile*, vol. 9, 1985.

Written by leading researchers into Chile's marine resources, this is the most
recent detailed account, with supporting data, of the country's fishing industry.

Together with forestry, that industry has been the most dynamic growth sector of the Chilean economy in recent years and is part of a deliberate attempt to reduce the country's dependence on copper for foreign exchange.

448 **Chile's national interest in the oceans.**
Victor A. Gallardo. Santiago: Institute of International Studies, University of Chile, 1976. 110p. (Special Publications Series, no. 10).

A meticulous study of the extent to which Chile has made use of the resources of its seas, suggesting that there is scope for much further exploitation, provided that conservation and pollution issues are taken into acount. The rapid growth of the fishing industry in the 1970s and 1980s indicates that Chilean business has taken the point, but this is still a useful survey.

449 **Chile sees big future in fisheries.**
N. Proudfoot. *Fishing News International*, no. 17 (Oct. 1978), p. 18-19.

Chile possesses some of the richest fishing waters in the world but only in the last decade has it begun to exploit their potential for export markets. In 1975, it stood seventeenth in the world ranking of tonnage catch; within ten years, it had risen to fifth. This short but informative article provides the background to that development.

450 **The water resources of Chile. An economic method for analyzing a key resource in a nation's development.**
Nathaniel Wollman. Baltimore, Maryland: Johns Hopkins University Press, 1968. 279p. bibliog. map.

Based on field research, this is an exhaustive survey of Chile's water supplies and their uses, which include irrigation, government projects and industrial and agricultural needs. The book also has methodological implications for similar studies in the future.

451 **Three important hydro projects in Chile.**
Mario Aguilar. *Water Power*, (May 1973), p. 161-65.

Chile has the highest per capita hydroelectric potential of any country in the world and this has been tapped increasingly since the 1940s. This is a good description of three power plants which were under construction at the time of writing – Rapel, El Toro and Antuco. All are now on full stream.

452 **Actividad forestal.** (Forestry activities.)
R. Sánchez. Santiago: Instituto Geográfico Militar, *Colección Geografía de Chile*, vol. 14, 1986. 153p.

Up-to-date, illustrated and with a strong statistical base of seventy-six tables, this is an account of the fastest growing sector of the Chilean economy in the last ten years.

453 **The development of the Chilean *hacienda* system, 1850-1973.**
     Cristóbal Kay.   In: *Land and labour in Latin America. Essays on
     the development of agrarian capitalism in the nineteenth and
     twentieth centuries.* Edited by Kenneth Duncan, Ian Rutledge, with
     the collaboration of Colin Harding. Cambridge: Cambridge
     University Press, 1977, p. 103-39.

A well-researched investigation of the dominant feature of the countryside in
Chile, the great estate, from its hey-day in the middle of the last century to its
radical reform in the 1970s, some of which has since been reversed. This is a neat
and well substantiated summary of the subject.

454 **Conflict and cooperation among Chilean sectoral elites.**
     Jean Carriére.   *Boletín de Estudios Latinoamericanos y del
     Caribe.* vol. 19 (1975), p. 16-27.

The author looks at the National Society of Agriculture (SNA) between 1932 and
1964, considering its role as a powerful lobby for the landowning élite in Chile, at
a time of considerable social and economic change. The result is useful as a study
of élite behaviour in situations where conflict between sectional and national
interests developed.

455 **The monetarist experiment in the Chilean countryside.**
     Cristóbal Kay.   *Third World Quarterly*, vol. 7, no. 2 (April 1985),
     p. 301-22.

A valuable survey, by a Chilean specialist on agrarian issues, of the main changes
in the country's rural society and economy since the military came to power in
1973.

456 **La política agraria del gobierno militar.** (The agrarian policy of the
     military government.)
     Cristóbal Kay.   *El Trimestre Económico*, vol. 48, no. 191
     (summer 1983), p. 567-601.

This is a heavily critical study of the agrarian policies of the Pinochet régime,
indicating how far the land reforms of the previous socialist government have
been changed since 1973.

457 **Destruction of the natural vegetation of north-central Chile.**
     Conrad J. Bahre.   Berkeley, California: University of California
     Press, 1979, 117p. bibliog. (University of California Publications in
     Geography, vol. 23).

A valuable factual study, of interest to geographers and conservationists. Based
on field-work, and well-illustrated, it documents the despoliation of virgin
territory in Coquimbo in northern Chile by methods of land use, originating five
hundred years ago, and continued to the present day by the region's peasantry.

Agricultural reform

458 **Landowners and politics in Chile: a study of the Sociedad Nacional de Agricultura (National Society of Agriculture), 1932-1970.**
Jean Carrière.   Amsterdam: Centre for Latin American Studies and Documentation, 1981. 245p. (CEDLA Incidental Publications, no. 18).

Though published rather earlier than the work on the same subject by Thomas C. Wright entitled *Landowners and reform in Chile. The Sociedad Nacional de Agricultura (National Society of Agriculture), 1919-1940* (q.v.), this is a thorough investigation of the Society's relationship with politics and attitudes to agrarian reform in Chile. It is a valuable contribution which both complements T. C. Wright's book and offers an interesting comparison with it, particularly concerning the 1930s.

459 **Chile's experiments in agrarian reform.**
William C. Thiesenhusen.   Milwaukee, Wisconsin: University of Wisconsin Press, 1966. 230p. bibliog. (Land Tenure Center, Land Economics Monographs, no. 1).

A pioneering work on Chilean land reform down to the mid-1960s, based on an analysis of four farms in the Chilean central valley. It offers an excellent introduction to the subject, but has been overtaken by events such as Frei's agrarian reforms, and more rapid changes under Allende and the military government's reconstitution of agricultural property after 1973. It is, notwithstanding, one of the best studies in English of the earlier period.

460 **The politics of land reform in Chile, 1950-1970.**
Robert R. Kaufman.   Cambridge, Massachusetts: Harvard University Press, 1972. 321p. bibliog.

A valuable historical study of the evolution of land reform programmes in Chile, prior to the advent of Popular Unity with its more drastic approach, which was ultimately disastrous, at least from the economic point of view.

461 **Agrarian reform in Chile.**
Jeannine Swift.   Lexington, Massachusetts: D. C. Heath, 1971. 125p. bibliog.

Written in the aftermath of the agrarian reform law passed by the Frei administration, this short study concentrates on the implications of that law and its likely effects. Though it is now heavily dated, its description of the process as it was going on has historical value.

462 **Agrarian reform and rural revolution in Allende's Chile.**
Peter Winn, Cristóbal Kay.   *Journal of Latin-American Studies and World Affairs*, vol. 6, part 1 (May 1974), p. 135-59.

Though written from a left-wing point of view, and based largely on official printed sources, this is a useful short summary of the progress and repercussions of agrarian reform under the Popular Unity government.

463 **Agrarian change after Allende's Chile.**
Cristóbal Kay.   In: *Chile after 1973: elements for the analysis of military rule*. Edited by David E. Hojman. Liverpool: Centre for Latin American Studies, University of Liverpool, 1985, p. 97-113. (Monograph Series, no. 12).

One of a series of short essays in the monograph edited by D. E. Hojman (q.v.), this is a succinct account by a Chilean specialist on agrarian affairs since the miltary coup of 1973, which is highly critical of the policies of the Pinochet régime. A useful summary, if the bias is recognized.

Science and technology

464 **Science and technology in Latin America.**
Edited by Christopher Roper, Jorge Silva.   London, New York: Longman, Latin American Newsletters Ltd., 1983. (Longman Guide to World Science and Technology).

One of a series intended to provide coverage of world scientific and technological institutions, this exhaustive listing of those in Latin America includes a good section on Chile (p. 58-74). The section for each country has a short introductory essay, giving basic data and notes on both public and private scientific policy. All institutions listed, which include universities, are accompanied by descriptive notes, but, unfortunately, not by addresses.

465 **El desarrollo científico y tecnológico en Chile. Un analisis cualitativo, 1965-86.** (Scientific and technological development in Chile. A qualitative analysis, 1965-85.)
Santiago: Corporación de Promoción Universitaria, 1987. 221p.

A detailed, up-to-date discussion and evaluation of the subject, ranging over demand and supply factors, finance, education, the role of government, a discussion of the various Chilean bodies involved in training for development and, finally, the transfer of technology from abroad. An important survey.

466 **Chile mira hacia las estrellas. Pequeña historia astronómica.** (Chile looks to the stars. A short astronomical history.)
Arturo Aldunate Phillips.   Santiago: Editorial Nacional Gabriela Mistral, 1975. 266p.

It is not generally known that the semi-desert region of northern Chile, the capital of which is La Serena, has some of the world's major astronomical laboratories, where, for about four-fifths of the year, the skies are cloudless. After a rather irrelevant essay on Chilean history in general (p. 1-111), the author describes and discusses the evolution of astronomical science in Chile, with good illustrations of the four observatories in the region (p. 111-266). These include the impressive Inter-American Observatory, which has the largest telescope in the southern hemisphere. Outside specialist journals, there is little information on the subject, and this book is a useful guide for the Spanish-speaking reader.

Language and Linguistics

467 **Spanish pronunciation in the Americas.**
  D. Lincoln Canfield.   Chicago: University of Chicago Press, 1981.
  118p. bibliog.
A basic work on Spanish American dialectology, with country-by-country surveys,
including one of Chile. There is a splendid and extensive bibliography of over 300
titles.

468 **Introducción al estudio del español de Chile.** (Introduction to the
  study of Chilean Spanish.)
  Ambrosio Rabanales.   Santiago: Universidad de Chile, Instituto
  de Filología, 1953. 146p.
The author deals with the concepts of 'Americanisms', the specific use of words in
particular Spanish-speaking countries of America such as Argentina and Peru,
and 'Chileanisms', those that are essentially used in Chile. A useful and
interesting book.

469 **La lengua castellana en Chile.** (The Spanish language in Chile.)
  Rodolfo Oroz.   Santiago: Universidad de Chile, 1966. 541p.
A fundamental book for the study of Spanish in Chile.

470 **Diccionario del habla chilena.** (A dictionary of Chilean
  pronunciation.)
  Santiago: Academia Chilena. Editorial Universitaria, 1978. 260p.
  bibliog.
An excellent lexicon, the prologue of which deals with the pronunciation of
Chilean Spanish and indicates that many words presumed to be peculiarly Chilean
often derive from other Latin American countries.

115

Language and Linguistics

471 **Diccionario ejemplificado de chilenismos y de otros usos
diferenciales del español en Chile.** (Illustrative dictionary of
Chileanisms and of other distinctive usages of Spanish in Chile.)
Felix Morales Pettorino, Oscar Quiroz Mejías, Juan Peña
Alvarez.   Valparaiso, Chile: Academia Superior de Ciencias
Pedagógicas, 1983-84. 4 vols.

An extraordinary undertaking recording all words known to be specifically
Chilean, including the particular meanings of Spanish words as well as the rich
vernacular of Chile, with its regional variations and many words derived from
aboriginal tongues.

472 **Diccionario de voces del norte de Chile.** (Dictionary of voices of the
north of Chile.)
Mario Bahamonde Silva.   Santiago: Editorial Nascimento, 1978.
400p. bibliog.

The Norte Grande (Great North) region of Chile consists largely of the Atacama
desert, barren in appearance but incredibly rich in minerals, mainly nitrates and
copper. The economic history of Chile has turned for over a hundred years on the
axis of their exploitation. This book, concerned with the terminology of the
region, place-names, mining terminology and distinctive folkloric expressions, not
only reveals the more recent past but also shows the influence of aboriginal Indian
cultures.

473 **Diccionario comentado mapuche-español y vocabulario español-
mapuche.** (A critical Mapuche-Spanish and Spanish-Mapuche
dictionary.)
E. Erize.   Buenos Aires: Universidad del Sur, 1960. 550p.

This is undoubtedly the best and most complete bilingual dictionary of the native
Indian language of Chile, that of the Mapuche, and Spanish which superseded it.

Folklore

474 **Folktales of Chile.**
Edited by Yolando Pino-Saavedra, translated from the Spanish by
Rockwell Gray.   Chicago: University of Chicago Press, 1967.
317p. (Folktales of the World Series).

This is a translated selection of the three-volume collections of the Chilean
author, published in 1960-63, with an introduction by Richard M. Dorson on new
folk traditions of Chile and the world. The selection includes animal tales, tales of
wonder, romantic legends and stories about tricksters and is an excellent
introduction to Chilean folklore.

475 **Geografía del mito y la leyenda chilenos.** (Geography of Chilean
myth and legend.)
Oreste Plath.   Santiago: Editorial Nascimento, 1973. 454p.

A considerable anthology of Chilean myth and legend culled from oral, printed
and literary sources, and arranged by geographical origin. The author is an
outstanding authority on Chilean popular culture.

476 **Folklore chilena.** (Chilean folklore.)
Oreste Plath.   Santiago: Editorial Nascimento, 1979. 492p.
bibliog.

An excellent compilation of various types of Chilean folklore by an acknowledged
authority. The eleven chapters cover most aspects of the field, such as traditions,
sayings, games, childrens' songs, and so on and each has its own bibliography.

Folklore

477 **Folklore médico chileno: antropología y salud.** (Chilean medical
folklore: anthropology and health.)
Oreste Plath.   Santiago: Editorial Nascimento, 1981. 331p.
bibliog.

A detailed survey of Chilean folklore on medical matters, both of Indian and
Spanish origin, this looks at traditional cures for a variety of afflictions.

Literature

General

478 **Chile. Anthology of new writing.**
Edited by Miller Williams. Kent, Ohio: Kent State University
Press, 1968. 1 vol. [n.p.]

Concerned with the writing of the Chilean generation after Neruda, this covers
poetry, short stories, an interview and a play. There are many translations by
Williams, who is himself a poet. A useful introduction and anthology.

479 **Modernismo in Chilean literature: the second period.**
John M. Fein. Durham, North Carolina: Duke University Press,
1965. 167p.

This short study is chiefly concerned with two literary reviews and the work of
Francisco Contreras (1877-1933), a Chilean poet and critic who lived in Paris for
the last thirty years of his life. He was a disciple of the Nicaraguan writer, Rubén
Darío, one of Latin America's leading poets of the late nineteenth and early
twentieth centuries and the founder of the modernist movement. Contreras's
own work is little known but he was the leading Chilean representative of that
movement.

480 **Chilean literature in Canada.**
Edited by Naín Nómez. Ottawa, Ontario: Ediciones Cordillera,
Ottawa Chilean Association, 1982. 247p.

A bilingual (English and Spanish) collection of poetry and short stories written by
Chilean exiles from the Pinochet régime now living and writing in Canada. The
content is very variable, but it is an interesting testimony of the capacity of
refugee intellectuals to continue their work.

Biographies and criticisms of novelists and novels

481 **Chilean society as seen through the novelistic world of Alberto Blest Gana.**
Victor M. Valenzuela.   Santiago: Talleres de Arancibia Hermanos, 1971. 157p. bibliog.

Blest Gana (1830-1920) is generally regarded as the founder of the Chilean novel. His prolific output was not affected by his varied career – as a soldier, a member of Congress and a diplomat who, at one time, served in London and Paris. His best-known novel, frequently re-printed, is *Martín Rivas* (q.v.), a classic portrayal of Chilean social life in the nineteenth century, which first appeared, in serial form, in 1862. This book is a useful study of his work, concentrating on his portrayal of the society and the aristocracy of his time.

482 **Juan Godoy.**
Thomas Edgar Lyon Jr.   New York: Twayne, 1972. 161p. bibliog. (Twayne's World Authors Series, no. 189).

Godoy (1889-1957) a novelist and short story writer of the 1940s and 1950s, is little known outside Chile. This is a sympathetic study of the man and his work.

483 **Eduardo Barrios.**
Ned Davison.   New York: Twayne, 1970. 152p. bibliog. (Twayne's World Authors Series, no. 125).

Though few people outside the Spanish-speaking world are aware of his work, Barrios (1884-1963) was an interesting Chilean novelist and playwright, who had an extremely varied career as both businessman and public servant. This biography, which deals with his work as well as his life, discusses the evolution of his writing, much of which reflects the Chilean environment.

484 **Metaphysics and aesthetics in the works of Eduardo Barrios.**
John Walker.   London: Tamesis, 1983. 190p.

Not so much a biography as a critical study of a Chilean writer, regarded by the author as a neglected master of fiction.

485 **Luis Durand.**
Donald M. Decker.   New York: Twayne, 1971. 179p. bibliog. (Twayne's World Authors Series, no. 118).

Luis Durand (1895-1954) was an interesting Chilean fiction writer in the 'regionalist' tradition, depicting, primarily, rural landscapes and life. His masterpiece is *Frontera* (Frontier) which looks at the nineteenth-century settlement of Indian Araucania and was published in 1949.

120

486 **José Donoso.**
George R. McMurray.   Boston, Massachusetts: Twayne, 1979.
178p. bibliog. (Twayne's World Authors Series, no. 517).

José Donoso (1924-   .) is, perhaps, Chile's most distinguished living novelist, whose writing reflects his contempt for upper-class Chilean society and his liking for surreal forms of expression. His most outstanding novel to date, *El obsceno pájaro de la noche* (The obscene bird of night) (q.v.) is particularly powerful in its language and imagery, both reflecting a profoundly pessimistic attitude towards the human condition.

487 **Juan Marín-Chilean. The man and his writings.**
James O. Swain.   Cleveland, Tennessee: Pathway Press, 1971.
224p. bibliog.

Although trained as a doctor, Juan Marín (1900-63) was a prolific writer of fiction, poetry, essays and travel accounts, who, despite his output, is little known outside Chile. This survey of his life, philosophy and writings is a useful introduction for the English-speaking world to the remarkably wide-ranging work of this Chilean author.

488 **Nicomedes Guzmán. Proletarian author in Chile's literary generation of 1938.**
Lon Pearson.   Columbia, Missouri: University of Missouri Press, 1976. 285p. bibliog.

The subject of this well-researched study, which is a synthesis of biography, criticism and literary history, was a well-known Chilean writer of the 1930s and 1940s, noted for his realistic portrayal of Chilean lower-class life. This is an excellent study of a neglected Chilean writer.

489 **The lost rib: female characters in the Spanish Amerian novel.**
Sharon Magnarelli.   Cranbury, New Jersey: Associated University Presses, 1985. 277p. bibliog.

An interesting study of the portrayal of women in eight well-known Latin American novels, written largely by men. Chile is represented by José Donoso's *Obsceno pájaro de la noche* (*Obscene Bird of Night*) (q.v.) (p. 147-68). The writer looks at his portrayal of women as witches and makes an interesting contribution.

490 **The boom in Spanish American literature: a personal history.**
José Donoso, translated from the Spanish by Gregory Kolovakos.   New York: Columbia University Press in association with the Center for Inter-American Relations, 1977. 122p.

A much needed translation of an inside view of the new Latin American novel, by one of its outstanding exponents.

Novels and short stories in translation

491 **Martín Rivas.**
Alberto Blest Gana, translated from the Spanish by Mrs Charles
Whitham. New York: Alfred A. Knopf, 1918. 431p.
This is probably the best-known Chilean novel of the last century, a classic which
realistically depicts society at mid-century.

492 **The partner.**
Jenaro Prieto, translated from the Spanish by Blanca de Roig, Guy
Dowler. London: Butterworth, 1931. 255p.
Prieto (1889-1946) has the reputation of being, perhaps, Chile's outstanding
humorist, though, unfortunately, most of his very amusing essays on Chilean life
and society have not yet been translated into English. This novel (*El socio*)
appeared in 1928. It is the satirical tale of a businessman who invents a partner
who then becomes increasingly 'real', to the point that his inventor commits
suicide, leaving the police to search for the partner who is held to be his
murderer.

493 **The devil's pit and other stories.**
Baldomero Lillo, edited and translated by Esther S. Dillon, Angel
Flores. Washington, DC: Pan American Union, 1959. 152p.
(UNESCO Collection of Representative Works of Latin American
Literature).
Lillo (1867-1923) may be regarded as the Zola of Chilean fiction for his graphic
social realism and his treatment of the appalling conditions under which the
Chilean working-classes, especially the coal-miners of the south, earned their
living. (The author's father was a miner.) This collection includes stories from two
of his most powerful works, *Sub terra* (Under ground) and *Cuadros mineros*
(Mining scenes). Lillo was one of the first Latin American authors to examine the
terrible effects of industrialization on working people.

494 **Brother Asno.**
Eduardo Barrios, translated from the Spanish by Edmundo García
Girón. New York: Las Americas, 1969. 134p.
El hermano asno, which might be defined as a psychological novel, first appeared
in 1922. It is based on monastic life, and contrasts two Franciscans, who are both
affected, in different ways, by carnal thoughts.

495 **Mirror of a mage.**
Vicente Huidobro, translated from the Spanish by Warren B.
Wells. Boston, Massachusetts: Houghton-Mifflin, 1931. 185p.
Huidobro's reputation rests largely on his outstanding poetry and his intellectual

122

Literature. Novels and short stories in translation

influence on Latin American letters as a whole. However, his novels are also full of interest. The original title of this work, written in Paris in the early 1920s and published in 1926, was *Cagliostro; novela-film* (Cagliostro; novel-film). It reflects his interest in the silent screen and shows the strong influence of the cinema in his narrative.

496 Portrait of a paladin.
Vicente Huidobro, translated from the Spanish by Warren B. Wells. New York: Horace Liveright, 1932. 316p.

This is the poet's interpretation of the life and times of Spain's greatest mediaeval hero.

497 The house of mist.
María Luisa Bombal, translated from the Spanish and enlarged by the author. New York: Farrar-Straus, 1947. 245p.

This novel is an expansion of the original, which first appeared in 1935, as *La última niebla* (The last mist). The writer (1910- .) employs a highly lyrical style. This contrasts with what one might call the common Chilean fictional modes of neo-realism and *criollismo*, that Latin American movement which emphasized popular culture and regional themes. This is a story of a married woman who lacks true love. Stylistically, the writer has been compared with Virginia Woolf.

498 The shrouded woman.
María Luisa Bombal, translated from the Spanish by the author. New York: Farrar-Straus, 1948. 198p.

An extraordinarily subjective novel, first published in 1938 as *La amortajada*, it describes, in flash-back, the analysis of various characters in a woman's mind, the woman herself being dead.

499 La Quintrala.
Magdalena Petit Marfán, translated from the Spanish by Lulú Vargas Vila. New York: Macmillan, 1942. 190p.

La Quintrala was the popular name given to Doña Catalina de los Ríos, a member of the rich Lisperguer family at the end of the sixteenth century. She had the reputation of being the Lucrezia Borgia of Chile and was involved in a number of scandals, including murder and a dubious involvement with Alonso de Ribera, then governor of Chile. She ended her life in a convent. This novel, by a well-known Chilean authoress, is based upon her extraordinary life.

500 Lautaro.
Fernando Alegría, translated from the Spanish by Delia Goetz. New York: Farrar & Rinehart, 1944. 176p.

First published in 1943 as *Lautaro, joven libertador de Arauco*, the novel is a fictional account of the great Araucanian chief, who fought the Spaniards in the sixteenth century and remains, in a sense, a national hero. Alegría (1918- .) is a novelist, poet and literary critic with a considerable and fascinating output who deserves much wider acclaim.

Literature. Novels and short stories in translation

501 **My horse González.**
Fernando Alegría, translated from the Spanish by Carlos Lozano.
New York: Las Américas, 1964. 187p.

A picaresque novel reflecting the author's experiences of Latin Americans in California, particularly San Francisco, stressing cultural differences. Alegría knows that part of the United States well, having studied and taught there.

502 **Born guilty.**
Manuel Rojas Sepúlveda, translated from the Spanish by Frank Gaynor. New York: Library Publishers, 1955. 314p.

Originally published in 1951 as *Hijo de ladrón* (Son of a thief), this is a powerful novel of social realism about the poor who, deprived of other opportunities, become delinquents. Rojas (1896-1973) might be seen as an existentialist writer in his later novels including this one which exercized considerable influence on others.

503 **Jemmy Button.**
Benjamin Subercaseaux, translated from the Spanish by Mary de Villar, Fred de Villar. London: W. H. Allen, 1955. 299p.

A remarkable historical novel, based on actual events. Captain Robert Fitzroy of HMS *Beagle* was commissioned, in 1830, to chart the coasts around Tierra del Fuego. There he took on board four Indians, three male and one female, who were christened Jemmy Button, York Minster, Boat and Fuegia Basket. Boat died soon after reaching England but the other three were placed with a clergyman's family and subsequently presented at court. They learned English but remained Indian and in 1833 went back to Tierra del Fuego on the *Beagle*, in the company of Charles Darwin. The writer evokes the episode, using imaginative material such as invented diaries but does not deal with the *dénouement* – Jemmy's murder of Anglican missionaries some years later and Fitzroy's suicide in 1865.

504 **Coronation.**
José Donoso, translated by Jocasta Goodwin. London: The Bodley Head, 1965. 262p.

The original Spanish version of Donoso's powerful novel was published in 1957, and won the William Faulkner Foundation Prize in 1962. It is the novel which established the author's reputation as an international literary figure. A scarcely-veiled attack on the Chilean aristocracy, it is the story of a ninety-four-year old widow of a Chilean politician who is slowly dying in Santiago and her middle-aged grandson who falls for the niece of one of her former maids who herself loves someone else. Like all Donoso's novels, it has an air of surrealism.

505 **This Sunday.**
José Donoso, translated by Lorraine O'Grady Freeman. New York: Knopf, 1967. 177p.

First published in 1965 as *Este domingo*, the novel is concerned with the relations between the poor and the rich and presents a scathing attack on the latter. This is not one of Donoso's surrealist novels but is, as usual, a book that is well worth reading. It centres on an old-fashioned middle-class family, in conflict with the changes of modern society. The different generations each speak in their own idiom.

506 **The obscene bird of night.**
José Donoso, translated from the Spanish by Hardie St. Martin, Leonard Mades. London: Jonathan Cape, 1974. 438p.

First published in Spanish in 1970, when the author lived in Spain, and initially translated into English in the United States in 1973 (by the same translators), this is Donoso's most powerful novel to date. The scene is set in a decrepit Catholic retreat house in Santiago, peopled by curious characters. The narrator is a deaf and dumb man, former secretary to a rich landowner, and the entire novel is written in vivid and surrealistic tones. An excellent translation of a very disturbing and original work of fiction. See also *The lost rib: female characters in the Spanish American novel* (q.v.).

507 **Sacred families.**
José Donoso, translated by Andrée Conrad. London: Victor Gollancz, 1978. 206p.

These three novellas by Chile's leading novelist are fantastic in the original sense of the word; macabre tales which have been well translated to capture Donoso's extraordinary mastery of language.

508 **A house in the country.**
José Donoso, translated from the Spanish by David Pritchard, Suzanne Jill Levine. London: Allen Lane, 1984. 352p.

First published in Spanish in 1978, then in English, in this translation, in 1983 in the United States, this is a characteristic novel by Chile's leading contemporary writer. It is concerned with the large family of the Venturas who retreat every year to their country seat and portrays the rituals they perform. It is, in fact, a biting indictment of the Chilean landed aristocracy. The author's prose style is individual and not easy to translate. However, this translation is excellent.

509 **I dreamt the snow was burning.**
Antonio Skármeta. London: Readers International, 1985. 220p.

Originally published in Spanish in 1975, this novel deals with working-class struggle in Chile through the story of a young football player aspiring to be a star. The action takes place in the months before the coup of 1973 and turns on the clash between individual ambition and collective consciousness, portraying, in almost parabolic style, the fight between unfettered free enterprise and democratic socialism.

510 **The house of the spirits.**
Isabel Allende, translated by Magda Bogin. London: Jonathan Cape, 1985. 368p.

A remarkable first novel by a niece of Salvador Allende, this is a picture of modern Chilean social and political development, presented through a family saga, culminating in the coup of 1973. A brilliantly written and vivid story.

511 **Of love and shadows.**
Isabel Allende, translated from the Spanish by Margaret Sayers Peden. London: Cape, 1987. 274p.

Isabel Allende's second novel to be translated into English has the same magical yet realistic style as her first, *The house of the spirits* (q.v.), though here the scene is contemporary. The story concerns the investigation, by the leading two characters, into the disappearance of a strange adolescent girl and clearly draws its inspiration from such widespread happenings in the dictatorial states of Latin America. The translation is excellent.

512 **Chilean writers in exile.**
Edited by Fernando Alegría. Trumansburg, New York: Crossing Press, 1982. 162p.

This is a collection of short novels by seven authors, edited by a doyen of Chilean writing. All the writers are in exile from the Pinochet régime, and, apart from their intrinsic interest as works of literature, their works also reveal that Chilean cultural life can be sustained, even outside the country.

513 **The copper nail: a story of Atacama.**
C. J. Lambert. London; Glasgow: Blackie, 1960. 144p. 2 maps.

A charming tale of an Indian boy in the Huasco valley, where the author himself farmed for many years, an experience recorded in *Sweet waters* (q.v.). This story relates how the boy grows up, marries and becomes prosperous but then meets disaster when his harvest fails. It has a happy ending, however, when, from a map given to him by a dying Indian, he discovers buried treasure. A well-written story which will appeal to children of both sexes.

Biographies and criticisms of poets and poetry

514 **The world and the stone: language and imagery in Neruda's *Canto general*.**
Frank Reiss. London: Oxford University Press, 1972. 170p. bibliog.

A detailed critical analysis of the highest quality of Neruda's best-known poem, or, rather, collection of poems under a generic title, inspired by the poet's feelings for Chile and for Latin America. An excellent bibliography and onomastic index are also provided in a work which is essential reading for the study of this part of Neruda's enormous output.

515 **Pablo Neruda. All poets the poet.**
Salvatore Bizzarro.   Metuchen, New Jersey: Scarecrow Press,
1979. 192p. bibliog.
An outstanding study of Neruda's life and work, including fascinating transcriptions of interviews conducted in Chile, especially with Neruda's widow, Matilde. The bibliography is first-rate.

516 **Earth tones. The poetry of Pablo Neruda.**
Manuel Durán, Margery Safir.   Bloomington, Indiana: University
of Indiana Press, 1981. 200p. bibliog.
One of the best critical studies of the finest modern poet writing in Spanish. It is a detailed critique of his life and work and includes some fascinating photographs of Neruda at different times and in a variety of places. The bibliography is extensive.

517 **Pablo Neruda: the poetics of prophecy.**
Enrico Mario Santí.   New York, London: Cornell University
Press, 1982. 256p. bibliog.
An important critical study of several of Neruda's best-known works, in which the author argues that Neruda's Marxist ideology does not conflict with his central position in the Western literary tradition, nor with his universal role as 'the poet as seer'.

518 **Pablo Neruda.**
Marjorie Agosín, translated from the Spanish by Lorraine Roses.
Boston, Massachusetts: Twayne, 1986. 157p. bibliog.
A critical study, by a Chilean poetess and literary critic, of the major themes in some of Neruda's best-known writings. Though adulatory in tone, it is an interesting and evocative critique and is well translated. It includes a chronology of Neruda's life and a very useful, though selective, bibliography.

519 **Memoirs.**
Pablo Neruda, translated from the Spanish by Hardie St. Martin.
Harmondsworth, England; New York: Penguin, 1978. 370p.
An excellent translation of the fascinating memoirs of the prolific and outstanding Chilean poet, who was also a prominent political figure in the Communist party, and diplomatic representative. Quite indispensable for the non-Spanish reader who wishes to understand the man and the poet.

520 **Passions and impressions.**
Pablo Neruda, translated by Margaret Sayers Peden.   New York:
Farrar, Straus & Giroux, 1978. 396p.
Really a sequel to Neruda's memoirs (q.v.), this book is a fascinating collection of his prose writings, recording his travels, his political activities as a Communist, comments on places and events and his relationships with other literary figures. Most of the entries, though quite short, are also vivid. This comes highly recommended.

Literature. Biographies and criticisms of poets and poetry

521 **Vicente Huidobro. The careers of a poet.**
René de Costa. Oxford: Clarendon, 1984. 186p. bibliog.
Huidobro (1893-1948) was, undoubtedly, one of Chile's and Latin America's most outstanding, prolific and influential writers. Much of his life was spent in France which he regarded as his first country. This carefully researched biography and critique, containing some interesting photographs, is an excellent study of his very varied career.

522 **Gabriela Mistral.**
Margaret J. Bates. *The Americas*, vol. 3, no. 2 (1946), p. 168-89. bibliog.
A combination of biographical notes and literary criticism, this is a succinct introduction to Chile's outstanding woman poet, illustrated with extracts from her work.

523 **Gabriela Mistral: the poet and her work.**
Margot Arce de Vásquez, translated by H. M. Anderson. New York: Gotham Library, New York University Press, 1964. 158p. bibliog.
A useful biography of the noted Chilean writer and Nobel prize-winner for literature, by a close personal friend. It is an intimate recollection of Gabriela Mistral's activities as a writer, diplomat, teacher and voyager.

524 **Gabriela Mistral's religious sensibility.**
Martic C. Taylor. Berkeley, California; Los Angeles: University of California Press, 1968. 191p. bibliog.
A sensitive and well-researched study of the religious element in the work of the poetess.

525 **Pedro Prado.**
John R. Kelly. New York: Twayne Publishers, 1974. 154p. bibliog. (Twayne's World Authors Series: Chile. no. 304).
Prado (1886-1952) was not only an architect, judge, painter and diplomat but also a poet of no mean stature, though his work has been nelgected. He also wrote novels, mostly with regional settings. An important intellectual influence, this is a sympathetic presentation of his life and work.

526 **The antipoetry of Nicanor Parra.**
Edith Grossman. New York: New York University Press, 1975. 201p. bibliog.
A valuable critical study of the work of this enigmatic poet, whose designation of his work as 'antipoetry' has been a subject of much literary debate. He uses colloquial Araucanian and Latin language and his work is highly individual. This is an excellent book for anyone wishing to become familiar with the poet and his work.

Poetry in translation

527 **La araucana.** (Araucania.)
Alonso de Ercilla y Zúñiga. Complete edition prepared by Olivo
Lazzarín Dante, with a preliminary study by Eduardo Solar
Correa. Buenos Aires: Editorial Francisco de Aguirre, 1977.
618p. (Collección Reino de Chile).

Ercilla y Zuñiga (1533-94), a Spanish nobleman, who took part in the campaigns
in south-central Chile against the Araucanian Indians, later wrote what is
generally regarded as the finest epic poem in Spanish, brilliantly describing the
landscapes of Chile, the wars that were fought and the Indians who fought them.
This is an edition based upon the hitherto standard one, that of José Toribio
Medina, published in 1916, and is a reliable text with some illustrations. There is
no satisfactory English translation but the title must be included here.

528 **The heights of Macchu Pichu.**
Pablo Neruda, translated by Nathaniel Tarn.   London: Jonathan
Cape, 1966. 47p.

One of the most famous and certainly one of the finest of the longer poems of
Neruda, beautifully translated, with an introduction by the leading British
authority on Neruda, Robert Pring-Mill, whose valuable preface is full of insight.
For those who do not know Spanish but wish to become aware of Neruda's art,
this is a very good book with which to begin.

529 **The early poems.**
Pablo Neruda, translated by David Ossman, Carlos B. Hagen.
New York: New Rivers Press, 1969. 98p.

A good translation of the lesser known poetry of Neruda in which the later,
greater works are clearly foreshadowed. The book is enhanced by illustrations by
Lucas Johnson, helpful notes and a biographical description.

530 **Selected poems: a bilingual edition.**
Pablo Neruda, edited, with a brief introduction, by Nathaniel
Tarn; translations from the Spanish by Nathaniel Tarn, Anthony
Kerrigan, W. S. Merwin, Alastair Reid.   New York: Delacorte
Press, 1972. 509p. (A Delta book).

This representative collection of Neruda's poetry down to 1967 is probably the
best bilingual collection in print, despite the inevitably uneven quality of the
translations. It is highly recommended.

531 **Extravagaria.**
Pablo Neruda, translated by Alastair Reid.   London: Jonathan
Cape, 1972. 303p.

First published in Spanish in 1958, this collection of some of Neruda's most

129

personal poetry reflects not only his command of language and rhythm but also his very individual thought. This bilingual edition of the almost untranslateable title is a valuable contribution to the understanding of Neruda and his poetry.

532 **Pablo Neruda: a basic anthology.**
Selection and introduction by Robert Pring-Mill.   Oxford: Dolphin, 1975. 218p.

This is an excellent compilation from Neruda's voluminous output by the leading British authority on the outstanding Chilean poet and Nobel prize-winner. It is enhanced by the compiler's biographical and critical introduction, based, not least, on his personal friendship with the poet.

533 **Isla Negra, a notebook.**
Pablo Neruda, translated from the Spanish by Alastair Reid, with an afterword by Enrico Mario Santi.   New York: Farrar, Straus & Giroux, 1981. 414p.

This collection of 102 poems takes its name from the place on the Pacific coast of Chile where Neruda lived, in general, from the early 1960s. It is, in effect, an autobiography in verse, paralleling his memoirs in prose. This is an outstanding translation, true to the spirit as well as the words themselves.

534 **Selected poems of Gabriela Mistral.**
Edited and translated from the Spanish by Doris Dana.
Baltimore, Maryland: Johns Hopkins University Press, 1971. 235p.

This is a useful, though not first-rate, translation of some of the poetry of the celebrated Chilean poetess and winner of the 1945 Nobel prize for literature. Mistral was the first Latin American writer to receive that honour. Though a number of her most striking poems are omitted, there is some compensation in the illustrations, woodcuts by Antonio Frasconi.

535 **The selected poetry of Vicente Huidobro.**
Edited and with an introduction by David M. Guss.   New York: New Directions, 1981. 234p.

This is a useful bilingual selection of some of Huidobro's characteristic poetry, written originally in both Spanish and French. Nine translators, including the editor, were involved in producing the compilation.

536 **Selected poems.**
María Elvira Piwonka, translated from the Spanish by Edward Newman Horn.   New York: Osmar Press, 1967. 61p.

A small collection of the mature work of a Chilean poetess who is, undeservedly, little known outside her own country.

537 Emergency poems.
Nicanor Parra, translated from the Spanish and with an
introduction by Miller Williams. New York: New Directions,
1972. 154p.

A physicist by profession, Parra (1914-   .) is probably second only to Neruda as
Chile's most important contemporary poet. His work is difficult to translate but
this typical collection is an excellent attempt.

538 Sermons and homilies of the Christ of Elqui.
Nicanor Parra, translated by Sandra Reyes. Missouri, St. Louis:
University of Missouri Press, 1984. 105p. bibliog.

During the 1920s and 1930s, years of great social distress in Chile, an itinerant
preacher, Domingo Zarate Vega, believing he had a mission from God, preached
throughout the country. The great modern poet, Parra, here puts into
characteristic verse the imagined utterances of Zarate.

539 This endless malice. Twenty-five poems.
Enrique Lihn, selected and translated by William Witherup, Serge
Echeverría. Northwood Narrows, New Hampshire: Lillabulero
Press, 1969. 82p.

Not an easy poet to comprehend, Lihn is, nevertheless, well-served by his
translators in this short, characteristic collection.

540 The dark room and other poems.
Enrique Lihn, translated from the Spanish by Jonathan Cohen,
John Felstiner, David Unger, edited by Patricio Lerzundi. New
York: New Directions, 1978. 147p.

Lihn's early poetry was highly romantic, but this collection reflects a more
colloquial style and is one of the few English translations of his work.

Art and Architecture

541 **Apuntes sobre arquitectura colonial chilena.** (Notes on Chilean colonial architecture.)
Roberto Dávila Carson, selection, introduction and design by Oscar Ortega, Silvia Pirotte. Santiago: Universidad de Chile, Facultad de Arquitectura y Urbanismo, Departamento de Diseño Arquitectónico, 1978. 273p. bibliog.

Between about 1920 and 1926, Dávila made around 200 careful drawings of Chilean colonial buildings, many of them domestic. This collection of the paintings not only splendidly reproduces them but also gives much ancillary information about them. A valuable contribution for historians, architects, art specialists and those interested in the preservation and restoration of historical buildings.

542 **Historia del arte en el reino de Chile.** (History of art in the kingdom of Chile.)
Eugenio Pereira Salas. Santiago: University of Chile, 1965. 497p.

This magnificently produced and well-illustrated book, by one of Chile's outstanding cultural historians, is, without doubt, the standard work on the subject.

543 **Raíces de una ciudad: Santiago, siglo XVI-XIX.** (Roots of a city: Santiago, sixteenth to nineteenth centuries.)
Santiago: Mar del Sur for the Banco de Santiago, 1980. 73p.

Prepared by two well-known historians, Carlos A. Cruz and Fernando Silva Vargas, this luxurious book traces the evolution of Chile's capital, from its foundation in 1541 to the beginning of the nineteenth century. The text is in Spanish but the lavish illustrations will please the non-Spanish-speaking reader.

132

544 **Historia de la pintura chilena.** (History of Chilean painting.)
Antonio Romero, with the collaboration of Fernando Aránguiz.
Santiago: Editorial Andrés Bello, 1976. 4th ed. 224p.

A very useful directory of over 300 Chilean painters, arranged by schools, from
Gil de Castro in the early nineteenth century to the present day.

545 **South American folk pottery: traditional techniques from Peru,
Ecuador, Bolivia, Venezuela, Chile, Colombia.**
Gertrude Litto.   New York: Watson-Guptill Publications, 1976.
224p. bibliog. maps.

The section of this beautifully illustrated book concerned with Chile (p. 75-85)
concentrates on the folk pottery of Pomaire and Quinchamalí, dealing with
craftsmen and craftswomen in these two famous centres of the art. There is also
useful technical data. A short but instructive article for those interested in
ceramics.

546 **The art of Chile.**
The Studio, vol. 139, no. 686 (May 1950), p. 130-60.

A special issue of the well-known art magazine, which contains essays by
distinguished Chilean scholars on the historical evolution of the fine arts, colonial
architecture, contemporary painting and sculpture, folk art and contemporary
architecture of the country. Lavishly illustrated, it provides a summary
introduction to the subject, up to the time of publication.

547 **Latin among lions: Alvaro Guevara.**
Diana Holman Hunt.   London: Michael Joseph, 1974. 313p.

A biography of one of Chile's leading contemporary artists.

548 **Veinte pintores contemporáneos de Chile.** (Twenty Chilean
contemporary painters.)
Victor Carvacho Herrera.   Santiago: Departamento de Extensión
Cultural del Ministerio de Educación, 1979. 78p. (Colección
Historia del Arte Chileno).

An excellent introduction to contemporary Chilean art, with very good
illustrations. The section on the outstanding Chilean artist, Matta, is particularly
good.

549 **La pintura en Chile desde la colonia hasta 1981.** (Painting in Chile
from the colonial period to 1981.)
Gaspar Galaz, Milan Ivelic.   Valparaiso: Universidad Católica de
Valparaiso, Ediciones Universitarias de Valparaiso, 1981. 393p.
bibliog.

An outstanding and lavishly illustrated survey of Chilean art from the colonial
beginnings to virtually the present day. It includes valuable interpretive essays as
well as biographies of artists, but the non-Spanish reader will still find it useful

because of the wealth of illustrative material, which includes photographs of modern artists, exhibitions and so on, as well as splendid reproductions in colour.

550 **Art in Latin America today: Chile.**
Antonio R. Romera. Washington, DC: Pan-American Union, 1963. 76p. bibliog.

A concise summary of modern Chilean art, with illustrations in black and white, by a well-known authority.

551 **Chile cultural. (Chilean culture).**
Santiago: Ministro de Relaciones Exteriores, Departamento de Asuntos Culturales, 1986. 75p.

A bilingual (English-Spanish) introduction to Chilean arts, well-illustrated, and with an introduction by the then Minister of Foreign Affairs and university professor, Jaime del Valle.

Music

552 **Los orígines del arte musical en Chile.** (The origins of the art of music in Chile.)
Eugenio Pereira Salas.   Santiago: Imprenta Universitaria, 1941. 374p. bibliog.

Written by Chile's leading cultural historian of this century, himself the husband of a distinguished singer and teacher, this is the most comprehensive history of Chilean music to date, covering the period from pre-Spanish times to the early twentieth century. It provides a complete inventory of compositions between 1714 and 1860 and other relevant material such as a list of musicians, transcriptions and illustrations.

553 **Historia de la música en Chile.** (History of music in Chile.)
Samuel Claro Valdés, Jorge Urrutia Blondel.   Santiago: Editorial Orbe, 1974. 192p. bibliog.

Claro is the doyen of Chilean musicologists and his collaboration with Urrutia has produced an outstanding synthesis and introduction to the music of Chile throughout its history. The knowledge of both authors is reflected in the bibliography, of almost 200 items.

554 **La creación musical en Chile, 1900-1951.** (Musical creation in Chile, 1900-1951.)
Vicente Salas Viu.   Santiago: Ediciones de la Universidad de Chile, [n.d.] 477p. bibliog.

A detailed panorama of musical evolution in Chile in the first half of this century, which is, in part, a social history. It considers the role of musical societies, and the part played by universities and provides, in addition, biographies of some forty composers and descriptions of their compositions.

135

555 **Historial de la cueca.** (Case study of the cueca.)
   Pablo Garrido.   Valparaíso: Ediciones Universitarias de
   Valparaíso, 1979. 245p. bibliog. map.

The cueca, or zamacueca, is Chile's national folk-dance which has its origins in
the colonial period. This is a well-illustrated, if somewhat rambling account of its
evolution, by a well-known authority on the subject. The illustrations include
cartoons, drawings, photographs of composers and also musical examples. The
bibliography is extensive, including a large number of press articles on the cueca
by the author.

556 **Música compuesta en Chile, 1900-1968.** (Music composed in Chile,
   1900-1968.)
   Roberto Escobar, Renato Yrarrázaval.   Santiago: Ediciones de la
   Biblioteca Nacional, 1969. 256p.

More narrowly focused than the work by V. Salas Viu (q.v.), though covering
some of the same ground, this is a more useful guide to all the compositons
produced in Chile during the period covered. It provides brief biographical notes
on the composers and has a useful index. The work is divided into sections by
musical type, such as orchestral works, chamber music, choral works and songs. It
is a very useful compilation.

557 **Víctor, an unfinished song.**
   Joan Turner Jara.   London: Jonathan Cape, 1983. 278p.

Written by his widow, this is a graphic and moving biography of one of Chile's
most popular singers and song-writers, dealing particularly with Víctor Jara's
important role in Chilean popular culture from the 1950s to the overthrow of
Allende in 1973. Jara was killed after the military coup, being a staunch supporter
of the Popular Unity government.

558 **Víctor Jara: his life and songs.**
   Víctor Jara.   London: Elm Tree Books in association with Essex
   Publishing, 1976. 127p.

Compiled by his widow, Joan Turner Jara, together with Ted Hicks and with a
foreword by the folk-singer Pete Seeger, this is a selection of thirty-two of Jara's
best-known songs, which also includes much other material on the Chilean
popular artist. His songs are part of standard repertory in the 'new Latin-
American song' movement, to which exile groups, such as Inti Illimani and
Quilapayún, belong.

559 **La nouvelle chanson chilienne.** (The new Chilean song.)
   Jean Clouzet.   Paris: Editions Seghers, 1975. 259p.

A valuable study of the popular musical social protest movement of the 1960s and
1970s, which survives strongly, though now mostly through exile groups. The
introductory essay traces the rise of the movement, with emphasis on the folkloric
origins of the songs and the role of the great popular singer, Violeta Parra. The
rest of the book consists of a large collection of lyrics, with texts in Spanish and
French. An interesting book for those concerned with studies of popular culture.
It also contains discographies to the date of publication.

560   **Violeta Parra and *la nueva canción chilena*.** (New Chilean song.)
Albrecht Moreno.   *Studies in Latin American Popular Culture*,
vol. 5 (1986), p. 108-27.

An excellent short study for the non-Spanish speaking reader, it describes and
discusses, with a good deal of insight, the celebrated folk-singer's key role in the
growth of Chilean 'protest' music, prior to the coup of 1973.

561   **El libro mayor de Violeta Parra.** (The major book of Violeta
Parra.)
Isabel Parra.   Madrid: Ediciones Michay, SA, 1985. 221p.

Compiled by her sister, this is a splendid evocation of the outstanding Chilean
folk-singer and composer. It contains many of her letters, poems and illustrations
and a discography and is an excellent all-round view of a remarkable artiste.

562   **Décimas.** (Ten-line stanzas.)
Violeta Parra.   Barcelona: Editorial Pomaire, 1970. 213p.

Violeta Parra (1917-67) was one of Latin America's most influential song-writers
and singers of the twentieth century, whose work as a collector of folk-music,
composer and artiste was outstanding. This extraordinary autobiography, written
in a traditional verse form of five verses of ten lines each, consists of ninety-two
poems, and is remarkably evocative.

Theatre and Cinema

563 The development of the national theatre in Chile to 1842.
Margaret V. Campbell. Gainesville, Florida: University of
Florida Press, 1958. 77p. (Latin American Monograph Series of
the School of Inter-American Studies, no. 4).

A useful short survey of the beginnings of the theatre in Chile, emphasizing key
figures such as José Joaquín de Mora and Andrés Bello, with interesting data on
particular plays and productions.

**564 Historia del teatro en Chile desde sus orígines hasta la muerte de
Juan Casacuberta, 1894.** (A history of the theatre in Chile from its
origins to the death of Juan Casacuberta, 1894.)
Eugenio Pereria Salas. Santiago: Ediciones de la Universidad de
Chile, 1974. 440p.

Written by Chile's outstanding cultural historian of the twentieth century, this is
an exhaustive history of Chilean theatre from pre-conquest ritual to the death on
stage of the romantic actor, Juan Casacuberta. The book is a mine of information,
culled from an extraordinary range of sources and embellished with numerous
illustrations, including cartoons and programmes. An appendix lists the plays
performed in Chile from 1612 to 1849.

565 Panorama del teatro chileno 1841-1959 (Estudio y antología).
(Panorama of Chilean theatre 1841-1959. A study and anthology.)
Julio Durán Cerda. Santiago: Editorial del Pacífico, 1959. 373p.
bibliog.

The introduction to this anthology is a valuable study of Chilean theatre from
1842 and the lively intellectual environment in which, apparently, theatre began
to show signs of real development. The anthology includes good examples to

138

illustrate the move away from works that were generally imitative of European trends to those, beginning with the dramas of Daniel Barros Grez in the late nineteenth century, that dealt with truly Chilean themes with characters recognizably drawn from Chilean life. Writers represented, in addition to Barros Grez, are Carlos Bello, Daniel Caldera, Domingo A. Izquierdo, Armando Moock and Antonio Acevedo Hernández.

566 **El teatro chileno de mediados del siglo XX.** (The Chilean theatre in the mid-twentieth century.)
Elena Castedo Ellerman. Santiago: Editorial Andrés Bello, 1982. 240p.

A thorough study of what was one of the richest periods of Chilean theatre, 1955-70. The author interprets the major trends in Chilean drama – realism, folklorism, the theatre of the absurd and Brechtian and workshop theatre – seeing each style as a response to the search for a genuine Chilean means of dramatic expression, dealing with indigenous characters and themes. There is also a useful biographical appendix of the authors dealt with in the book.

567 **Behind Spanish American footlights.**
Willis Knapp Jones. Austin, Texas; London: University of Texas Press, 1966. 609p. bibliog.

This historical overview of Spanish American theatre, in this century, is valuable in that it puts Chilean theatre into a wider perspective. The chapters specifically on Chile deal with the development of its theatre to 1841, the period from 1842 to the 1930s, and the period from 1941 to 1961. This is a most useful survey.

568 **El teatro chileno contemporáneo (1941-1973).** (Contemporary Chilean theatre, 1941-1973.)
Teodosio Fernández. Madrid: Editorial Playor, 1982. 213p. bibliog.

A useful study of a rich period in Chilean theatre, with a welcome look at neglected writers of the 1940s and early 1950s, as well as of comedies and musicals and a short but commendable study of 'popular' theatre, an area of much conflict.

569 **La dramaturgia chilena: 1960-1970.** (Chilean play-writing: 1960-1970.)
María de la Luz Hurtado. Santiago: CENECA, 1983. 111p.

The writer is one of the most prolific commentators on Chilean theatre. This valuable study examines theatre in the 1960s, in the social and political context of rapid social change, political radicalization and a cultural environment that was becoming more and more politicized.

570 **El teatro chileno actual.** (Modern Chilean theatre.)
José Ricardo Morales. Santiago: Editora Zig-Zag, 1966. 310p.

This work considers nine plays written in the 1950s and 1960s. The author's introduction – followed by the texts – provides biographies of the writers. Of equal interest are the resumés, by each of them, of his or her approach to the theatre. The plays selected are the earliest products of what is known as the 'university generation', dating from the founding of university theatres in the 1940s, which had a profound effect on subsequent developments in Chilean drama.

571 **Dramatists in revolt. The new Latin American theatre.**
Leon F. Lyday, George W. Woodyard. Austin, Texas; London: University of Texas Press, 1976. 275p. bibliog.

Dealing with Latin American drama of the 1960s, this book contains chapters dealing with three Chilean writers: Jorge Díaz (p. 59-76), Luis Alberto Heiremans (p. 120-32) and Egon Wolff (p. 190-201). All three chapters give excellent introductions to the authors, by George Woodyard and Margaret Sayers Peden.

572 **El teatro de Juan Radrigán (11 obras).** (The theatre of Juan Radrigán. Eleven works.)
Juan Radrigán. Santiago; Minnesota: CENECA and the University of Minnesota Press, 1984. 418p.

Chile's most prolific contemporary dramatist presents here eleven characteristic works, in which the characters are people living at the margins of society – tramps, prostitutes, the poor. The plays are full of poetry and humour, and use many Chilean colloquialisms, for which a glossary – which is lacking – would have been helpful. Two critical essays on his work precede the texts.

573 **El cine de Allende.** (Allende's cinema.)
Francesco Bolzoni. Valencia: Fernando Torres, 1974. 163p.

A useful account of the 'new' cinema in the period of the Popular Unity régime.

574 **Chile: el cine contra el fascismo.** (Chile: cinema against fascism.)
Patrico Guzmán, Pedro Sempere. Valencia: Fernando Torres, 1977. 250p.

An excellent account of those Chilean film-makers in exile after the coup of 1973, considering their philosphies and films.

575 **Chilean cinema.**
Michael Chanan. London: British Film Institute, 1976. 102p. bibliog.

This book provides reprints of interviews, from European publications, on the cinema. The interviews were with several Chilean directors in exile from Pinochet's Chile. Also reprinted are articles from the press on Chilean films and a filmography is included. There is a sympathetic and intelligent introduction.

576 **Re-visión del cine chileno.** (Re-examination of Chilean cinema.)
Edited by Alicia Vega. Santiago: Editorial Aconcagua, 1979.
391p.

This is, in effect, the published result of a research project under the aegis of the *Centro de Indagación y Expresión Cultural y Artística* (CENECA), (Centre for Research and Cultural and Artistic Expression), in Santiago, Chile's most dynamic institution of its kind. The work deals with fictional films, from the silent era (1910-21) to that of sound (1934-79), and looks at characters and plots, dramatic construction and editing and acting. There is a section on documentary films and Part three is devoted to conclusions. An important study, produced under the degree of censorship which characterizes Pinochet's Chile.

577 **Cinema and social change in Latin America: conversations with filmmakers.**
Julianne Burton. Austin, Texas: University of Texas Press, 1986.
302p.

Three chapters of this fascinating book are devoted to Chile, comprising interviews with Patricio Guzmán (p. 49-68), Raul Ruíz (p. 181-94), and Nelson Villagra (p. 211-19). Villagra is an actor rather than a filmmaker, but all three contributors are exiles. All express their political as well as their artistic convictions in their interviews and statements.

Food and Wine

578 **La tía Pepa.** (Auntie Josie.)
   Santiago: Editora Zig-Zag, 10th ed., 1944. 348p.
This is a quite comprehensive collection of Chilean recipes which also gives wider
culinary advice and helpful tips on domestic hygiene.

579 **Cocina popular.** (Popular cooking.)
   Mariano Bravo Walker, revised by Julio Santa María Santa Cruz.
   Santiago: Editorial Universitaria, 1971. 327p.
For Spanish-readers, this is a useful compendium on Chilean cooking.

580 **Sabor y saber de la cocina chilena.** (Taste and knowledge of
   Chilean cooking.)
   Hernán Eyzaguirre Lyon.   Santiago: Editorial Andrés Bello,
   1987. 154p.
An interesting history of Chilean cooking, giving also some typical recipes.

581 **Chilean wine.**
   Jan Read.   London: Sotheby's Publications, 1987. 176p.
A guide to the increasingly popular wines of Chile which is illustrated excellently
with twenty-four colour and forty black and white pictures. The best wines of
Chile are among the finest in the world and exports have increased rapidly in
recent years. The book also includes a section on Chilean cooking by Maite
Manjón.

Sport and Recreation

582 **Chinganas (saloons), bailes máscaras, (masked balls) and the prensa chismosa (gossip press): three aspects of creole culture in nineteenth-century Santiago de Chile.**
Gertrude Matyoka Yeager. *Studies in Latin American Popular Culture*, vol. 1 (1982), p. 106-12.

Though a very short and largely descriptive piece, this gives a fascinating glimpse at three Chilean forms of recreation in the capital city last century. A welcome addition to the very sparse literature in English on Chilean creole culture, indicating what scope there is for a much larger work.

583 **Fútbol en Chile, 1895-1945.** (Football in Chile, 1895-1945.)
Fernando Larraín Mancheño. Santiago: Federación de Foot-ball (sic) de Chile, 1945. 67p.

Written to commemorate the first half century of Chilean football, by one who played a prominent part in it from his schooldays in the early 1900s, this is a fascinating history of the national sport with details of teams throughout the regional and the international scenes. The historical section highlights the significant role of the British community in Chile in the growth of football, emphasized by the names of many clubs.

Television and Radio

584 **La televisión y los sectores populares.** (Television and the popular
   sectors.)
   Michèle Mattelart, Mabel Piccini. *Comunicación y Cultura*
   Buenos Aires; Santiago: Editorial Galerna, no. 2 (Jan. 1978),
   p. 3-76.

A detailed examination, from a left-wing point of view, of the political use made
of television during the government of Popular Unity, to raise political
consciousness among the working-classes. It is based on case studies of three
working-class districts of Santiago.

585 **Políticas nacionales de comunicación.** (National communication
   policies.)
   Quito: Editorial Epoca, 1981. 660p.

Concerned with radio and television in Latin America, this compendium contains
a long essay (p. 339-407) on the Chilean scene, by Raquel Salinas Bascur,
describing the media and the legal framework in which they operate. Naturally,
under an authoritarian régime, the framework may be changed abruptly but this is
a useful exposition for the period it covers.

586 **Estudios sobre la televisión chilena.** (Studies on Chilean television.)
   Valerio Fuenzalida. Santiago: Corporación de Promoción
   Universitaria, 1984. 2nd ed. 207p.

A detailed and up-dated survey of television in Chile, which, in effect, is
summarized by E. G. McAnany (q.v.) in English. This much longer Spanish
exposition is, for those who use the language and are interested in the media, a
sine qua non.

587 **Cultural policy and television: Chile as a case.**
Emile G. McAnany. *Studies in Latin American Popular Culture*,
vol. 6 (1987), p. 55-67.

A most interesting survey of contemporary Chilean television, which emphasizes
the extent to which the medium has been increasingly subjected to government
regulation under the Pinochet régime and also how far both the content of
programmes and their cultural significance has changed. The conclusion is that
information and cultural and educational material has declined, while material
purely for entertainment, most of it imported, has increased. The author believes,
however, that there is still scope for the medium to become a national cultural
vehicle of communication, given certain policy changes.

Printed Media

588 **Creating a climate of opinion? the *Los Angeles Times* and Salvador Allende.**
Michael Gerald Greenfield. *Proceedings of the Pacific Coast Council on Latin American Studies*, vol. 5 (1976), p. 57-68.
A fascinating short study of how a leading North American newspaper sought to influence public opinion on the Chilean presidential election of 1970, opposing left-wing and centrist candidates alike.

589 **The comic book in a socialist society: Allende's Chile, 1970-73.**
Allen L. Woll. *Journal of Popular Culture*, vol. 9, no. 4 (1976), p. 1039-45.
Under Popular Unity, a deliberate attempt was made by the government to persuade artists to adopt a political position, notably to minimize American cultural influence. *La Firme*, a comic book promoted by the government, began in 1971: it satirized the Chilean upper classes and Americans, not least the CIA, portrayed as the villains of the piece. Though a piece of propaganda, it is valuable for the study of the period and, as the author indicates, shows how governments can seek to influence attitudes, even through comics.

590 **The Chilean press since Allende.**
Jerry W. Knudson. *Gazette: International Journal for Mass Communication Studies* (The Netherlands), vol. 27, no. 1 (1981), p. 5-20.
An objective appraisal of government conduct towards the mass media after the military coup of 1973. Though, as the author notes, some unsuccessful attempts were made to muzzle the press under the socialist régime of Allende, the repressive nature of its successor has led to a degree of self-censorship by the mass media which almost amounts to imposed censorship. Magazines tend to be more outspoken than the daily press, but they, too, must be cautious. It is based on secondary sources and interviews.

146

Museums and Libraries

591 **Chile.**
In: *The World of Learning*. London: Europa, 1987, 37th ed.
p. 287-96.
The section on Chile in this standard and comprehensive work of reference gives details of almost all relevant Chilean institutions – universities, libraries, museums, archives, learned societies, academies and so on, including reference to UN research institutes. It also includes the names of prominent people concerned with them.

592 **Museums in Latin America: Chile.**
Greta Mostny. *Museum* (UNESCO), vol. 25, no. 3 (1973).
p. 176-78.
A short descriptive guide by a leading Chilean archaeologist.

593 **A select guide to Chilean libraries and archives.**
Peter J. Sehlinger. Bloomington, Indiana: Indiana University, 1979. 35p. (Latin American Studies Working Papers, no. 9).
A short but excellent descriptive guide, which deals with the major libraries and archives, notably in Santiago, but also covers specialized libraries such as those of the Grand Masonic Lodge of Chile, of international organizations based there, for instance the Economic Commission for Latin America and some selected libraries in the provinces. A most useful tool for the researcher in Chile.

594 **The National Library in Chile, 1813-1978.**
Juan R. Freudenthal. *Libri*, vol. 28, no. 3 (Sept. 1978), p. 182-95.
One of Chile's most durable and valuable institutions, the Biblioteca Nacional is the equivalent, for that country, of the British Library or the Library of Congress. This is a concise survey of its history and importance in the national life.

Museums and Libraries

595 **Museo colonial de San Francisco.** (The colonial museum of San
Francisco.)
Isabel Cruz.   Santiago: Departamento de Extensión Cultural del
Ministerio de Educación, 1978. 78p. (Colección Museos Chilenos).

The San Francisco Church of Santiago, standing, prominent, on the city's main
thoroughfare, is one of Chile's most important colonial buildings, founded in
1572. It is now a national museum and this splendidly-illustrated book is an
excellent catalogue of its holdings.

596 **Museo chileno de arte precolombino.** (The Chilean museum of pre-
Columbian art.)
Carlos Aldunate del Solar.   Santiago: [n.p.] 1983. 85p.

The museum opened in 1981, the result of a collaborative effort between a private
collector of pre-Columbian Chilean material and the municipality of Santiago.
This is, in effect, a catalogue of the exhibits, well-illustrated and with
accompanying notes.

Newspapers in English and Professional Periodicals

597 **My not so golden newspapering days in wildest Chile.**
David Attlee Phillips. *The Smithsonian*, vol. 14, no. 3 (1983),
p. 104-21.

These are the reminiscences of the editor of the *South Pacific Mail*, the leading
English-language newspaper in Chile, from 1949 to 1954, which give useful
information on the origins of the paper and on its founder, Oswald Hardey
Evans.

598 **Américas.**
Washington, DC: Organization of American States, 1949- .
monthly.

Intended for the general reader, this well-illustrated magazine covers all the
American countries, and is published in English, Portuguese and Spanish.

599 **Hispanic American Historical Review.**
Durham, North Carolina: Duke University Press, 1921- .
quarterly.

Since its inception the *Review* has been published by Duke University Press.
However, its editorial offices move between important centres of Latin American
studies in the United States, and are currently at the University of Florida at
Gainesville. The pioneer journal, in English, on Latin American history, it has
retained its reputation for the quality of its articles and reviews in the scholastic
field, and is quite indispensable to historians and social scientists. A striking
feature in recent years has been the reports of conversations with distinguished
Latin Americanists from all over the world. Chile has been well-represented in its
coverage.

Newspapers in English and Professional Periodicals

600   **Journal of Latin American Studies.**
Cambridge: Cambridge University Press, 1969-   . semi-annual.
The leading British academic journal, published under the aegis of the national university centres in Latin American studies and edited from the London Institute. Multi-disciplinary in nature, it publishes scholarly articles with a strong emphasis on the social sciences and history. A major feature is the space allowed for book reviews, with review articles on specific themes. A number of important articles have been published on Chile, past and present, to which the cumulative index for the first fifteen volumes (1969-83), published in 1986, provides a good guide.

601   **Latin American Research Review.**
Albuquerque, New Mexico: Latin American Institute of the University of New Mexico for the Latin American Studies Association, 1965-   . three times per year.
The key multi-disciplinary journal on the state of continuing academic research on Latin America. Apart from survey articles, bibliographical essays and discussion papers, it also has a review section. It is quite essential for all scholars and students of Latin America.

602   **Bulletin of Latin American Studies.**
Oxford: Oxford Microform Publications, 1981-83. Oxford: Pergamon Press for the Society of Latin American Studies (UK), 1984-   . three times per year.
This scholarly journal arose from the growth of Latin American studies in British universities and the development of a national, professional association to promote those studies. Multi-disciplinary in aim, it publishes articles, many of contemporary interest, as well as book reviews. A number of important articles on Chile, particularly since 1970, have appeared in its pages.

603   **Latin American Theatre Review.**
Kansas: University of Kansas Press for the Center of Latin American Studies, 1967-   . bi-annual.
This useful periodical publishes articles, in English, Spanish and Portuguese, on the theatre in Latin America and includes reviews of theatre in the major centres, including Santiago. As well as quite frequent articles on the theatre in Chile, it also has notes on festivals and meetings, and book reviews.

604   **NACLA report on the Americas.**
New York: North American Congress on Latin America, 1967-   . bi-monthly.
The focus of this publication is the analysis of the implications of United States policies in Latin America and, while the articles it contains are often controversial and, perhaps, polemical, it offers a welcome provocative view of Latin American developments.

605 **Nueva Historia.** (New History.)
London: Institute of Latin American Studies for the Associación de Historiadores de Chile (Association of Chilean Historians), 1981- . quarterly.

Founded on the initiative of a group of Chilean refugee historians, this periodical has already acquired a reputation for serious historical study on Chile. It publishes research articles and reviews of a high quality, exclusively on Chilean topics. It is an increasingly important publication in Spanish for historians of that country.

606 **Latin American Regional Reports: Southern Cone.**
London: Latin American Newsletters, 1979. ten times per year.

A valuable report on current affairs, based on world-wide news sources and correspondents' reports from the different countries, this is one of the best vehicles for following contemporary events in Chile in political, economic, social and international spheres.

Bibliographies

General

607 Handbook of Latin American studies.
Gainesville, Florida: University of Florida Press, 1936- . annual.
Perhaps the most indispensable of all bibliographical tools on Latin America, the *Handbook* covers, in separate volumes, the humanities and the social sciences. General entries in different disciplines are followed by country surveys provided by recognized academic specialists; the individual entries are annotated and full details of publication provided. One of the most valuable aspects of this outstanding publication is its inclusion of periodical literature, in most relevant languages, as well as books. Currently, the respective volumes on humanities and social sciences appear in alternate years.

608 Accounts of nineteenth-century South America: an annotated checklist of works by British and United States observers.
Bernard Naylor. London: Athlone, 1969. 80p. (University of London. Institute of Latin American Studies Monographs, no. 2).
This excellent bibliography is divided into three chronological sections: 1800-30; 1830-70 and 1870-1900. Each section is sub-divided according to geographical regions, and contains every significant item on Chile published in English in that period. The annotations are concise but very informative.

609 Directory of libraries and special collections on Latin America and the Caribbean.
Bernard Naylor, Laurence Hallewell, Colin Steele.
London: Athlone, 1975. 141p. (Institute of Latin American Studies Monographs, no. 5).
This is an excellent guide to library collections on Latin America in the United

Kingdom, covering almost 150 libraries. Information is given on location, holdings, classification schemes and opening hours. The excellent subject index enables the prospective reader to identify the locations of the major holdings on Chile.

610 **Latin America: social science information sources 1967-79.**
Robert L. Delorme.   Santa Barbara, California;
Oxford: ABC-Clio, 1981. 262p.

An exhaustive listing of books and articles published during the indicated period. The section of Chile (p. 99-116) inevitably reflects the contemporary preoccupation with the fall of Allende and the military government from 1973. There is both an author and a subject index, each meticulously compiled.

611 **Latin American newspapers in United States libraries.**
Compiled by Steven M. Charno.   Austin, Texas; London: University of Texas Press for the Conference on Latin American History, 1968. 619p.

Although now, inevitably, somewhat dated, this union list is still valuable for the researcher, listing well over 5,000 Latin American newspapers in libraries in the United States. Until fairly recently, the Chilean press had the reputation of being a free press and its history, reflected in part in this list, indicates how strong that tradition was. The section devoted to Chile (p. 119-44) obviously includes much ephemera and short-lived papers but it also indicates where the longer-running ones (such as *El Mercurio* of Santiago, *El Diario Ilustrado*, a Catholic organ and others, reflecting particular views) may be found in repositories in the United States.

Subject

612 **Research guide to Andean history: Bolivia, Chile, Ecuador and Peru.**
Edited by John J. TePaske.   Durham, North Carolina: Duke University Press, 1981. 346p.

This extremely valuable compilation contains eleven contributions by distinguished Chileanists, each of whom provides not only a guide to the location of primary sources, in Chile, on various aspects of the country's evolution, but also extensive bibliographical references. The Chilean section covers over eighty pages (53-134) and no researcher interested in conducting historical work in Chile should neglect to consult it.

613 **Chile.**
Robert Oppenheimer. Los Angeles: Latin American Studies
Center, California State University, 1977. 91p. (Latin American
Bibliography Series).
A comprehensive bibliography on Chilean history since independence, covering
general works and the more specialized books on the period to 1920, then from
that date to 1970. The impact of the Allende and Pinochet periods on scholars is
indicated by the fact that about half the items listed relate to those régimes.

614 **Historical dictionary of Chile.**
Salvatore Bizzarro. Metuchen, New Jersey; London: Scarecrow
Press, 1987. 2nd ed. 583p. bibliog.
This is a welcome version, up-dated and much enlarged, of the original edition
which appeared in 1972. The bibliography (of almost fifty pages) is very useful,
ranging from ephemera in *Time* to more substantial works. It is quite
comprehensive and merits frequent reference, though the author's bias to
contemporary events is obvious and, perhaps, somewhat misplaced. For example,
Salvador Allende is given four and a half pages, Balmaceda almost one complete
page, though the historian of Chile might assert that, by the year 2000, the
Revolution of 1891 may be seen as more significant than the Revolution of 1973 in
the country's evolution. Furthermore, there are some curious omissions. This
writer could not find, for instance, a reference to Fransisco Nuñéz de Pineda y
Bascuñán, and an onomastic index might have been useful. Nonetheless, the
production of such a book is a daunting task, and the author *has* produced a very
valuable reference work.

615 **Chile.**
Carmen Cariola, Osvaldo Sunkel. In: *Latin America: a guide to
economic history, 1830-1930.* Edited by Roberto Cortés-Conde,
Stanley J. Stein. Berkeley; Los Angeles; London: University of
California Press, 1977, p. 273-363. bibliog.
A vital contribution to the field, commenting on almost every published work, the
chief repositories, and periodicals on Chilean economic history, with an
introductory essay on the country's development over the period surveyed. It is
quite indispensable for the historian and economist.

616 **A bibliography on South American economic affairs. Articles in
nineteenth-century periodicals.**
Tom B. Jones, Elizabeth Anne Warburton, Anne Kingsley.
Minneapolis, Minnesota: University of Minnesota Press, 1955.
146p.
A vital bibliographical tool for the economic historian of the continent, itemizing
entries from nearly 200 periodicals in English, French, Spanish, German and
Italian. A short general section, divided into categories such as 'trade' and
'finance', is followed by longer compilations organized by country. The entries,
including those for Chile (p. 90-105) are divided into several categories, including,
'agriculture', 'mining', 'labor' and so on.

617 **The historiography of the 'Portalian' period (1830-1891) in Chile.**
Simon Collier. *Hispanic American Historical Review*, vol. 57, no. 4 (Nov. 1977), p. 660-90.
An outstanding historiographical essay by the leading British authority on the period. The author surveys virtually all the significant works, many in Spanish, and offers the reader not only his own astute interpretation of nineteenth-century Chile but also trenchant suggestions for future research.

618 **A survey of recent Chilean historiography, 1965-1976.**
William F. Sater. *Latin American Research Review*, vol. 14, no. 2 (1979), p. 55-88.
An excellent and comprehensive survey of works published on Chilean history between the years indicated. The author, a well known historian of Chile in the United States, omits no article or book in his coverage.

619 **El impacto académico de los terremotos políticos: investigaciones de la historia chilena en inglés, 1977-1983.** (The academic impact of political earthquakes: research on Chilean history in English, 1977-1983.)
Paul Drake. *Alternativas*, no. 2 (Jan.-April 1984), p. 56-78.
An excellent survey of works, in English, on Chile in the period covered, listing virtually all the important titles, which include books, articles and doctoral dissertations. The bibliography itself is divided into disciplinary sections and is far from being confined to history.

620 **The Chilean revolution of 1891 and its historiography.**
Harold Blakemore. *Hispanic American Historical Review*, vol. 45, no. 3 (Aug. 1965), p. 393-421.
A seminal article on the different interpretations of a key event in modern Chilean history, drawing a distinction between 'economic' and 'constitutional' emphases in the chief works which had appeared by the time of writing and suggesting possible future lines of enquiry.

621 **Latin American politics: a historical bibliography.**
Gail A. Schlacter. Santa Barbara, California; Denver Colorado; Oxford: ABC-Clio, 1984. 297p.
An excellent guide to the field, with comprehensive coverage of relevant books and articles. The section on Chile (p. 188-206), while divided into chronological sections, concentrates on the period since 1970, and the annotations are both very informative and objective. There is a long subject index, an author index and a list of periodicals. Altogether, this is a valuable research tool.

622 **Visions of Chile.**
Arturo Valenzuela, J. Samuel Valenzuela. *Latin American Research Review*, vol. 10, no. 3 (1975), p. 155-75.
Written by the fraternity of two outstanding Chilean political scientists, this article

surveys, interprets and comments on over thirty books and articles on the military coup of 1973, looking at its causes and effects. Though all the items considered were published within two years of the event, the Valenzuelas' analysis of them is valuable and objective, classifying the works as politically leftist, centrist and rightist. Their 'visions' are neatly summarized and tabulated.

623 **The Allende years: a union list of Chilean imprints, 1970-1973, in selected North American libraries, with a supplemental holdings list of books published elsewhere for the same period by Chileans or about Chile or Chileans.**
Compiled by Lee H. Williams, Jnr. Boston, Massachusetts: G. K. Hall, 1977. 339p.
This represents a very valuable reference work.

624 **A bibliography of United States-Latin American relations since 1810.**
Compiled by David F. Trask, Michael C. Meyer, Roger R. Trask. Lincoln, Nebraska: University of Nebraska Press, 1968. 441p.
This is a key listing of works on the subject, down to the year of publication. It covers books, articles, dissertations, and so on, on United States relations with the continent and with individual countries.

625 **Supplement to a bibliography of United States-Latin American Relations since 1810.**
Compiled and edited by Michael C. Meyer. Lincoln, Nebraska: University of Nebraska Press, 1979. 193p.
Covering works since 1965, this up-dates the bibliography by David F. Trask *et al* (q.v.).

626 **Population research in Latin America and the Caribbean: a reference bibliography.**
Barry Edmonston. Ann Arbor, Michigan: University Microfilms International for the International Population Program and the Latin American Studies Program, Cornell University, 1979. 161p. (Monograph Publishing: Sponsor Series).
A useful listing of recent publications on demographic and anthropological research into Latin American and Caribbean demography. References are listed by country and such subject headings as general studies, distribution, fertility, marriage, mortality and migration.

627 **Guide to Latin American and West Indian census material: a bibliography and union list. Chile.**
Compiled by Carole Travis.   London: Institute of Latin American Studies, 1982. 32p.

This is the second in a series under the aegis of the Standing Conference of National and University Libraries through its Advisory Committee on Latin American Materials. It lists all known censuses taken in Chile, with locations of the material in British libraries and provides a subject index and a short bibliography. A valuable reference work on Chilean population throughout history.

628 **Historia bibliográfica de la novela chilena.** (Bibliographical history of the Chilean novel.)
Homero Castillo, Raúl Silva Castro.   Mexico City: Ediciones de Andrea, 1961. 214p. (Colección Studium, no. 28).

An exhaustive listing of Chilean novels of the nineteenth and twentieth centuries, to the date of publication. The authors are listed alphabetically and, although there are no commentaries, this is a valuable reference work.

629 **Index to anthologies of Latin American literature in English translation.**
Juan R. Freudenthal, Patricia M. Freudenthal.   Boston, Massachusetts: G. K. Hall, 1977. bibliog.

Arranged by author, with valuable translator and geographical indexes, this work indexes almost 120 anthologies and identifies over 1,200 Latin American authors. It is an excellent compilation.

630 **Chilean literature: a working list of secondary sources.**
David William Foster.   Boston, Massachusetts: G. K. Hall, 1978. 263p.

There is a very useful research tool for students of literature in Chile, covering some 300 journals and listing bibliographies, criticism and essays on almost 50 authors.

631 **Diccionario de la literatura chilena.** (Dictionary of Chilean literature.)
Efraím Szumelevicz.   Santiago: Editorial Andrés Bello, 1984. 2nd ed. 494p. bibliog.

A very comprehensive listing of Chilean authors, with biographical notes, publications and dates, a number of short literary essays and an extensive bibliography, which is a valuable tool of reference. Though ephemeral authors and works figure in its pages, it covers those of more lasting value as well.

632 **Alonso de Ercilla y Zúñiga: a basic bibliography.**
August J. Aquila. London: Grant & Cutler, 1975. 96p. (Research Bibliographies and Checklists, no. 11).

A very handy checklist of editions, translations and critical works on *La araucana* (Araucania), the outstanding epic poem on the conquest of Chile.

633 **A guide to the music of Latin America.**
Gilbert Chase. Washington, DC: Pan-American Union and the Library of Congress, 1962. 2nd ed. 411p.

Twenty-four pages (163-87) of this very useful guide are devoted to Chile. The compiler, an outstanding authority in the field, introduces the bibliographical items with a short but useful essay and, in the list, covers over 300 items. Some of these, however, are not strictly musicology, such as travel accounts which have references to Chilean music in them. Nevertheless, it is a valuable listing.

634 **Annotated bibliography of Latin-American popular music with particular reference to Chile and to nueva canción (new song).**
Jan Fairley. *Popular Music*, no. 5 (1985), p. 305-55.

A striking characteristic of modern Latin American culture, including that of Chile, has been the emergence of the 'new song' movement, much of which expresses popular protest against authoritarian régimes. While this article covers the entire continent, it contains a good deal of material specifically on Chile, including sections on such key Chilean performers and composers as Victor Jara and Violeta Parra. The annotations are excellent.

635 **Bibliografía del teatro hispanoamericano contemporáneo (1900-1980).** (Bibliography of the contemporary Spanish-American theatre, 1900-80.)
Fernando de Toro. Frankfurt: Verveurt Verlag Klaus, 1986. 2 vols.

The most comprehensive bibliography on the Spanish-American theatre to date, comprising 700 pages in all. Unfortunately, it lacks an index and a listing by country, which would have made it more useful. The first volume deals with original plays published in books, journals and anthologies, and has a list of translated works. The second volume deals with criticism.

636 **The new Latin American cinema. An annotated bibliography of sources in English, Spanish and Portuguese, 1960-1980.**
Julianne Burton. New York: Smyrna Press, 1983.

This useful compilation includes twenty-eight references to the Chilean cinema and Chilean film-makers (p. 20-21 and 54-59), notably on the Allende period and the work of artists in exile from the Pinochet régime.

Bibliographies. Subject

637   **Las relaciones laborales en Chile, 1810-1973.** (Labour relations in
      Chile, 1810-1973.)
      Alvaro Góngora Escobedo, Leonardo Bravo González.
      Dimensión Histórica de Chile, no. 2 (1985), p. 142-219.
This is an exhaustive listing of published work, in Spanish, on the subject, which
includes works translated from other languages. A useful subject index precedes
the impressive list of titles, but there are no annotations.

638   **Agrarian reform in Latin America: an annotated bibliography.**
      Compiled by the staff of the Land Tenure Center Library of the
      University of Wisconsin at Madison.   Madison, Wisconsin:
      University of Wisconsin Press, 1974. 667p.
Nearly 300 items in this impressive bibliography deal with Chilean issues (p. 246-
303). The annotations are sound and, while much has been published since on the
subject, this is an indispensable listing for those interested in agrarian reform in
Chile, when that issue became a national priority in the 1960s and 1970s.

639   **Bibliografía de la educación chilena, 1973-1980.** (Bibliography of
      Chilean education, 1973-1980.)
      Maria Clara Grossi, Ernesto Schiefelbein.   Santiago: Corporación
      de Promoción Universitaria, 1980. 335p.
A valuable annotated bibliography on works published in the period cited, with
entries classified by topic and author.

640   **Bibliografía sobre el impacto del proceso inmigratorio masivo en el
      cono sur de América. Argentina-Brasil-Chile-Uruguay.**
      (Bibliography on the impact of the massive immigration process in
      the southern cone of America. Argentina-Brazil-Chile-Uruguay.)
      Mexico: Instituto Panamericano de Geografia e Historia, 1984.
      207p. (Serie Inmigracion, vol. 1).
The work of numerous compilers, this exhaustive bibliography includes (p. 121-
87) a comprehensive listing of titles relating to Chile, for the period from
independence to 1930. The compilers, Juan Ricardo Couyoumdjian and Antonia
Rebolledo Hernández, have used titles in languages other than Spanish.

641   **Women in Spanish America: an annotated bibliography from pre-
      conquest to contemporary times.**
      Compiled by Meri Knaster.   Boston, Massachusetts: G. K. Hall,
      1977. 696p.
A useful bibliography on an ever-growing subject of interest to scholars. The
work is divided by periods and includes 2,534 entries, many relating to Chile,
where women have played a significant part in public life.

642 **Bio-bibliografía de la filosofía en Chile desde el siglo XVI hasta
1980.** (Bio-bibliography of philosophy in Chile from the sixteenth
century to 1980.)
Edited by Fernando Astorquiza Pizarro.   Santiago: Universidad
de Chile, Facultad de Filosofía, Humanidades y Educación,
Departamento de Bibliotecología, 1982. 295p.

A valuable collection of articles including bio-bibliographies on the periods 1500-
1818, 1818-1900 and 1900-80. Over 3,300 items are cited.

Statistics

643 **Anuario estadístico de América Latina.** (Statistical yearbook of
Latin America.)
Santiago: United Nations, Economic Commission for Latin
America and the Caribbean. 1973- . (United Nations Document,
E/CEPALC).

A basic source for such topics as social welfare and development, economic
growth, prices, public spending, foreign commerce, external debt and so on. In
short, an indispensable source of statistics for the countries of the region,
published in both Spanish and English.

644 **Statistical abstract of Latin America.**
Los Angeles: University of California, Center of Latin American
Studies, 1955- . annual.

A most valuable compilation, based on official sources, giving the essential figures
on population, society, economy, education and other topics.

645 **Historical statistics of Chile.**
Compiled by Markos J. Mamalakis.   Westport, Connecticut;
London: Greenwood, 1978-86. 5 vols. bibliog.

This extraordinary enterprise, the work of one scholar, is a basic reference tool
for anyone working on Chile. Based on the compiler's long experience of Chile,
as an economist and on his unrivalled knowledge of Chilean official statistics, the
first five volumes, in a series which is planned to run to eight, cover: *National
accounts* (vol. 1), *Demography and the labour force* (vol. 2), *Forestry and related
activities* (vol. 3), *Money, prices and credit services* (vol. 4) and *Money, banking
and financial services* (vol. 5). The average length of each volume is 400 pages or
more; each has an introduction to the theme, descriptive passages throughout,
many statistical tables and a comprehensive bibliography. The fruit of years of
research, the volumes that have appeared so far indicate what a mammoth
undertaking this is and are a fundamental source.

Indexes

There follow three separate indexes: authors (personal and corporate); titles; and subjects. Title entries are italicized and refer either to the main titles, or to other works cited in the annotations. The numbers refer to bibliographic entry rather than page numbers. Individual index entries are arranged in alphabetical sequence.

Index of Authors

166

Index of Titles

173

174

175

Index of Subjects

A

A. D. Bordes 164
Aarons, John
  traveller's account 56
Aborigines
  see Indians; Language
    and linguistics
Academies 591
Acevedo Hernández,
  Antonio (dramatist)
  565
Aconcagua River 80
Administrative reform
  maps 43
Aerial photographs 22
Agricultural reform 99,
  458-463
  bibliography 638
  economic effects 460
  politics of 458-463
  see also History; Names
    of individual
    governments
Agriculture 23, 453-457
  conflict of interests 454
  see also Farms; History;
    Land use; Names of
    individual
    governments; National
    Society of Agriculture;
    Politics; Sheep-farming
Air force 371
Airlines 429
  see also History
Alacaluf 16
Alegría, F. (novelist)
  in translation 500-501
Alessandri government
  (1958-64) 291
  economic development
  291
  Marxist analysis 291
  social structure 291
Alessandri, President Jorge
  see Alessandri
    government

Alessandri, President
  Arturo
  see History (Alessandri
    governments, 1920-25;
    1932-38); History
    (Alessandri, President
    Arturo)
Allende government
  (1970-73) 101, 186-201,
  360-361, 367, 372, 584,
  589, 614, 636
  agricultural reform 190,
    333, 456, 462
  aims 186
  and 'new' cinema 573
  and Mapuche 97
  and Movement of
    Revolutionary Left
    (MIR) 368
  and press (censorship)
    590
  and religion 279
  bibliographies 613, 618,
    623
  bureaucracy 358
  copper (expropriation of
    El Teniente mine) 438
  criticism of 199, 366
  culture 190
  economic development
    192, 291
  economic policies 400
  economic policies
    (income redistribution)
    401
  economic problems 400
  economics 190
  education policies
    320-321, 323
  foreign policy 223
  health and welfare
    policies 313
  housing policies 299-300,
    302-303
  faction fighting 197
  international setting 192
  ideology 190

Marxist analysis 291, 320
methods 196
ministers 192
mistakes 192, 197, 200,
  400
motor vehicle industry
  417-418
nationalization 416
neo-Fascism 177
newspaper reports 189
overthrow 189, 194, 201,
  320, 557
overthrow (role of USA)
  225, 383
penal system (local
  tribunals) 362
policies 187, 192, 196
politics 190
popular participation
  programme 337-338
progress 187
propaganda press 589
public expenditure
  (military) 379
relations with Cuba 228
relations with USA 190,
  196, 21, 224-225
relations with USSR 226
'road to socialism' 187, 362
social structure 291
statistics 191, 338
US ambassador 196
US economic pressure
  223
Allende, Isabel (novelist)
  in translation 510-511
Allende, President Salvador
  186
  see also Allende
    government
Alliance for Progress
  see Frei government
    (1964-70)
Ambassadors
  see Names of individual
    ambassadors, countries
    and governments

Diplomatic history
  see History (relations
    with)
Diplomatic relations
  see International relations
Domestic service
  see Women
Donoso, José (novelist,
    1924- .)
  biography 486
  criticism 486, 489
  in translation 504-508
Drama 100, 478, 570-571
  Brechtian 566
  characterization 565
  Chilean themes 565-566
  criticism 570
  folklorism 566
  indigenous characters
    565-566
  realism 566
  theatre of the absurd 566
  see also Names of
    individual dramatists
    and plays
Dundonald, Earl of
  see Cochrane, Lord
Durand, Luis (novelist,
    1895-1954)
  biography 485

E

Earle, John
  traveller's account 62
Earthquakes 24, 411
Easter Island 15
  see also Archaeology and
    archaeological sites;
    History
Ecology 76
  see also Conservation
Economic Commission for
    Latin America 593
Economic dependence 397
  see also History
Economic depression
    (1980s) 408, 413
  see also History (world
    depression)

Economic development 20,
    25, 192, 251, 257, 290,
    307, 390, 395-396, 399,
    401
  see also Chilean
    Development
    Corporation
    (CORFO); History;
    Names of individual
    governments; Names of
    individual industries,
    e.g. copper
Economic geography 21
Economic history
  see History (economic)
    and, e.g. History
    (inflation)
Economic institutions 1
Economic liberalism 382,
    399
Economic nationalism 397
Economic problems 34,
    289, 398
  effects on children 314
  see also Housing; Names
    of individual
    governments;
    Unemployment
Economics
  balance of payments 399
  budget (and bureaucracy)
    358
  costs 399
  exchange rates 399
  foreign capital 360
  indexation 309
  macroeconomic model
    398
  metallic standard 398
  monetary correction 309
  periodical 606
  protective tariffs 399
  public expenditure 379
  statistics 643, 645
  tax indexation (effects on
    inflation) 405
  trade flows 399
  see also Names of
    individual
    governments
Economy 23, 389-410
  export 395, 399

export (foreign-owned)
    396
  multinational
    corporations 397
  role of state 411
  sectoral development.
    395
  statistics 390, 395, 403,
    409, 644-645
  structure 390
  transition 403
  see also Agricultural
    reform; Fishing;
    Government policy;
    History; Industry, and
    names of individual
    industries, e.g.
    Minerals and mining;
    Inflation; Names of
    individual government;
    Nationalization;
    Regional economy;
    Stock-market;
    Urbanization
Education 315-326
  and labour 322
  and politics 317-321,
    323-324
  and repression 324
  bibliography 639
  curricula 320
  ideology 321
  international aid 316-317
  planning (as politics) 317
  problems 323
  reform 318, 320-321
  statistics 644
  see also Higher education;
    History; National
    unified school; Science
    and technology;
    Students; Universities,
    and names of individual
    universities; Women
Edwards, Jorge (diplomat)
    228
Egan, Patrick (US Minister
    to Chile) 211
El Algarrobo (open-cast
    mine) 442
El Diario Ilustrado 611
El Mercurio 611

183

History *contd.*
California gold rush
(1849) 248
Cape Horn 122
capitalism 101, 105, 140,163
Catholic Church 244, 276
Catholic University in
Santiago 244
chinganas (saloons) 582
Christian Democracy
period (1964-70)
182-185
Church-State relations
277-278
civil-military relations
107, 172, 175
civil war (1851) 104
civil war (1859) 104
civil war (1891) 103-104
class consciousness
334-335, 391
coal industry 142-143
colonial period 20, 110,
112, 114-123, 266-267
colonization (general)
247, 250, 254
Communism and
Communist party 217
composers (biographies)
554, 556
Congress 169
Congress (statistics) 348
conquistadores 114, 209
consensus tradition 351
conservatives 234
constitution 107, 133-134,
345
cooking 580
copper 146-147, 396,
432-433
copper (decline) 434
copper (El Teniente) 437
copper (large scale mines)
434-435, 437
creole culture 582
cueca 555
democracy 107, 237,
346-347
democratization 345
development 105, 112,
137, 158, 179, 253
dictatorships 172

dictionary of 614
documents 155-156
Easter Island
(annexation) 166
economic 29, 49, 104-105,
109-110, 112, 131-132,
134-135, 137-148, 152,
154, 158-163, 165-166,
170, 172-173, 179, 201,
350, 432-433
economic (bibliographies)
615-616
economic dependence
105, 112, 140, 159, 163,
170
economic development
396
economic modernization
393
economic structure 390
economic transition 394
economy (statistics) 390
education 232-234,
315-316, 322
electorate (statistics) 348
élites 160, 329
élitist political system
(impact on society)
347-348, 393
entrepreneurship 393
environment 166
ethnohistory 88, 92
export economy 396
extra-territorial
population (Chileans in
California) 248
Fascism 243, 257
fine art 546
football 583
foreign offices 155
folk-dance 555
forts and garrison towns
296
gold 248, 444
gun-running 169
haciendas (great estates)
453
health and welfare 311
heroism 242
Ibáñez government
(1927-31) 172
Ibáñez government

(1952-58) (expenditure)
379
ideology 231, 234, 238,
244
independence period
(1810-33) 44-45, 59,
108, 123-134
Indians 114, 118-119,
122
industrialization 179
industrialization (failure
of) 393
industry (general) 138
inequality 288
inflation (reactions to)
391
intellectuals 232-233,
236-242, 244, 329
international relations
155, 169, 204-215
iodine 162
Irisarri loan 131
journalism 233
Juan Fernández Islands
113
kinship 126, 286, 349
labour (bibliography) 616,
637
labour (working
conditions) 341
labour (railways) 425
labour (Yarur textile mill)
341
labour movement 327-328
labour movement 334-335
labour movement (and
national development)
335
labour movement (and
politics) 333
labour movement (and
populism) 336
labour movement (and
repression) 334
labour movement
(radicalization) 334
labour movement (urban)
335
labour movement
(Valparaiso maritime
strike of 1903) 334
land distribution 331, 333

landowners 165, 178, 390, 454
language and linguistics 233
law 233
left-wing parties 350
liberals 234
Lisbon earthquake (1755) 24
literary 233, 488
loans 131, 170
Magellan Straits 422
Magellan Straits (dispute with Argentina) 214
maps 41, 102, 294
migrants (economic impact) 249
migrants (German) 247, 253-255
migrants (nationalist reactions) 249
migrants (religious impact) 278
migrants (Yugoslav) 259
military 107, 152, 171-172, 175, 388
military coup (1924), 172
military (Prussianization) 171
minerals and mining 146-147, 154, 335, 432
minerals and mining (bibliography) 616
minority communities (African and Indian women)
minority communities (British) 260, 583
minority communities (contributions) 253-258, 260
minority communities (German) 253-254
minority communities (Jewish sephardic) 258
minority communities (non-Catholic) 278
minority communities (Yugoslav) 259
missionaries 277
monetary policy 389

music 552-554
music (and universities) 554
music (compositions) 552, 554, 556
music (transcriptions) 552
musical societies 554
musicians 552
Nacimiento 296
National Library of Santiago 240, 594
nationalism 211, 243
natural resources 393
navy 127, 129-130, 173, 211
Nazi party 181
neo-fascism 177
nitrates 151, 158-164, 168, 170, 210, 445
nitrate clippers 164
oral 341
Pacific ocean 122, 130, 141
packet-boats 422
painters 544, 549
Papacy 214
'parliamentary period' 347
Patagonia (dispute with Argentina) 214
periodicals 599-600, 605, 616
philology 232
philosophy 232-233
philosophy (bio-bibliography) 642
photographs and photography 149, 253, 294
poetry 157, 232-233
political 110, 123-124, 126, 132, 134, 136-137, 152, 158-160, 162, 166, 168, 172-201, 207, 231, 234, 238-239, 272, 345-351, 388, 391
political change 347
political parties 347
political parties (and public policy) 348
political parties (social support for) 347

political stability 345
politics and religion 276
politics (bibliography) 621
Polynesia 166
popular movement 350
Popular Unity period (1970-73) 97, 186-201
population and demography (fertility) 246
population and demography (marriage patterns) 246
population and demography (methodology) 245-246
population and demography (Petorca valley) 246
population and demography (primary records) 246
population and demography (regional) 246
populism 176, 336
'Portalian period' (bibliography) 617
positivism 236-237
postal service 422-423
prensa chismosa (gossip press) 582
presidency 351
presidents (Radical) 217
pressure groups 178, 288
pro-Church parties 234
proletariat 163
propaganda 169
prose-writing 233
protectionism 132, 165
Protestantism 277-278
public expenditure (statistics) 348
quasi-authoritarianism 345
race relations 117
Radical party 350
railways 424-425
railways (and economic development)
railways (statistics) 425
recreation in Santiago 582

photographs 521
poetry in translation 535
Human geography 28, 34
Human rights
  and religion 283-284
  Pinochet government 383,
    386-387
Hunters and hunting 100
Hydroelectricity
  potential 451
  power plants 451
  see also Antuco; El Toro;
    Rapel

I

Ibáñez del Campo, General
  Carlos 172
  see also History (Ibáñez
    government)
Ideology see Education;
  History; Names of
  individual
  governments,
  ideologies, e.g.
  Fascism, and political
  parties; Poetry
Illustrated London News 49
Imperial College, University
  of London see
  University of London
Indians 16-17, 78, 86, 89-90,
  92-99, 471-473, 485
  ethnohistory 92
  religion 95
  reservations 92, 94, 99
  social structure 94-96
  see also Alacaluf;
    Araucanians;
    Atacameño; History;
    Mapuche; Ona;
    Selk'nam; Yaghan
    (Yahgan); Yámana
Industrial development 420
Industrial relations 328-329
  see also Copper; Labour;
    Unions
Industrialization 23, 278,
  417
  see also History

Industry 411-421
  decentralization 420
  government policies 420
  import substitution 420
  multinational companies
    415
  see also Arica; Coal;
    Copper; History
    (industry) and, e.g.
    History (iodine); Motor
    vehicle; Names of
    individual
    governments; Nitrates;
    Oil; Television
Inflation 392, 398, 405
  see also History
Insects 68
  see also Coleoptera
Institute for Policy Studies
  375
Institute of Development
  Studies 187
Institute of International
  Studies of the
  University of Chile 203
Institute of Social Studies
  (The Hague) 192
Institutions see Social
  institutions; Political
  institutions; Economic
  institutions; Religion;
  Science and technology
Intellectuals 480
  see also History
Inter-American observatory
  466
Internal migration 251-252
International relations
  202-203
  periodical 606
  see also History
    (international relations)
    and, e.g. History
    (relations with Peru);
    Names of individual
    countries and
    governments
Iodine see History
Irisarri, Antonio José 131
  see also History (Irissari
    loan)
Iron see El Algarrobo

Islands 15-17, 28, 34, 38-39,
  61-62, 67, 72, 86, 90,
  100, 113, 122, 166
  see also Names of
    individual Islands, e.g.
    Easter Island
Izquierdo, Domingo A.
  (dramatist) 565

J

Jara, Victor (musician)
  and 'new song' movement
    58
  bibliography 634
  biography 557
  songs 558
Jewish minority
  communities 257-258
  see also History (minority
    communities)
Journalism see History
Juan Fernández Islands see
  History

K

Kennecott white paper 438
Kennedy, President 218
Kinship 285
  see also History
Körner, Emil 171

L

Labour 327-344, 413
  and politics 354, 360
  bibliography 637
  export industries
    (influence) 330
  statistics 645
  see also Education;
    History and, e.g.
    History (rural labour);
    Names of individual
    governments; Unions
Labour movement 339
  and politics 327-328, 333
  see also History; Names
    of individual
    governments; Unions

189

Middle Eastern minority
communities 256
Migrants and migration
247-252
bibliography 640
statistics 251
see also Archaeology and
archaeological sites;
History; History (extra-
territorial population);
Internal migration;
Minority communities;
Urban migration;
Women (and urban
migration)
Military 190
and politics 354, 379
intervention 376
role in development 369
study 376
thought 369, 376
see also Air Force;
Carabineros;
Civil-military relations;
History; Navy;
Pinochet government
Military academy 230
Military coup (1973) see
Pinochet government
Military Junta see Pinochet
government
Minas Blancas (copper
mine) 435
Minerals and mining
436-446
ENAMI (success of) 443
exports 431
geographical data 430
government explorations
431
imports 431
metal making 436
non-ferrous 436
open-cast 436
output 431
private investment 431
projects 431
reports 430
small-scale 443
statistics 430
technical aspects 430
terminology 472

see also Anaconda
Company; Atacama;
Coal; Coquimbo; Gold;
History (minerals and
mining) and, e.g.
History (copper); Iron;
Lithium; Molybdenum;
Nitrates; Oil; Silver;
United States of
America
Minority communities 16,
216, 253-260
see also British; German;
History; Jewish; Middle
Eastern
MIR see Movement of
Revolutionary Left
Missions and missionaries
17, 93
see also History
(missionaries)
Mistral, Gabriela (poet)
522-524
biography 522-523
criticism 522, 524
in translation 534
Moffit, Ronni
assassination 375
Molina, Enrique 237
Molluscs 68
Molybdenum 430
Moock, Armando
(dramatist) 565
Mora, José Joaquín de
and theatre 563
Moral codes
Mapuche 95
Motor vehicle industry
development 417-418
location 418
see also Names of
individual governments
Mountain peaks see Andes
mountain range
Mountaineering 32, 35-36,
62
Movement of Revolutionary
Left (MIR) 368
Museums 591-592
colonial museum of San
Francisco
pre-Columbian art 596

Music 552-562
and universities 554
bibliography 633
chamber 556
choral 556
composers (biographies)
556
compositions 556
cueca (zamacueca) 555
orchestral 556
photographs (of
composers) 555
songs 556, 558
songs (patriotic) 157
see also Folklore
(children's songs);
History (music) and,
e.g. History (cueca);
Names of individual
musicians; 'New song'
movement

N

Nacimiento
see also History
(Nacimiento)
National Library of
Santiago 594
see also History
National Society of
Agriculture 178, 454,
458
National unified school 320
Nationalism 185
see also History
(nationalism)
Nationalization 397
see also Names of
individual governments
and industries
Natural history 67
see also Fauna; Flora;
Names of individual
areas, e.g. Patagonia
Navy 371
see also History; Royal
Navy
Nazi party see History
Neruda, Pablo (poet)
514-520

Map of Chile

This map shows the more important towns and other features.

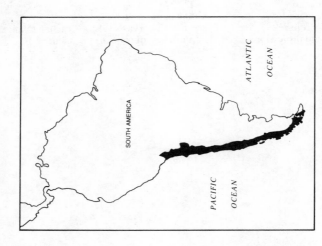

REGION NUMBER	REGION NAME	NAMES OF CORRESPONDING

PERU

BOLIVIA

ARGENTINA

A N D E S

A N D E S

ATACAMA DESERT

Arica

Iquique

Antofagasta

Copiapó

La Serena

Valparaiso

Santiago

Rancagua

I

II

III

IV

V

VI

SOUTH AMERICA

PACIFIC OCEAN

ATLANTIC OCEAN

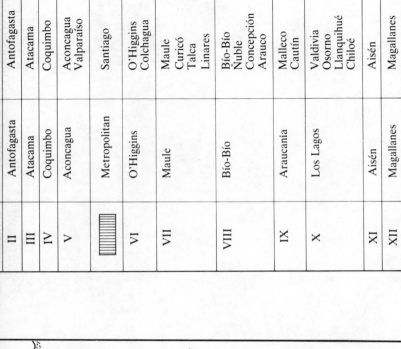

II	Antofagasta	Antofagasta
III	Atacama	Atacama
IV	Coquimbo	Coquimbo
V	Aconcagua	Aconcagua Valparaíso
(shaded)	Metropolitan	Santiago
VI	O'Higgins	O'Higgins Colchagua
VII	Maule	Maule Curicó Talca Linares
VIII	Bío-Bío	Bío-Bío Ñuble Concepción Arauco
IX	Araucania	Malleco Cautín
X	Los Lagos	Valdivia Osorno Llanquihué Chiloé
XI	Aisén	Aisén
XII	Magallanes	Magallanes

Iquique etc = Regional Capital